The Virtual Training Guidebook

How to Design, Deliver, and Implement Live Online Learning

Cindy Huggett

D1494617

ASTD

ASTD Press is an internationally renowned source of insightful and practical information on workplace learning, performance, and professional development.

ASTD Press
1640 King Street Box 1443
Alexandria, VA 22313-1443 USA

Ordering information: Books published by ASTD Press can be purchased by visiting ASTD's website at store.astd.org or by calling 800.628.2783 or 703.683.8100.

Library of Congress Control Number: 2013955127

ISBN-10: 1-56286-861-6
ISNB-13: 978-1-56286-861-1
e-ISBN: 978-1-60728-648-6

ASTD Press Editorial Staff:
Director: Glenn Saltzman
Manager and Editor, ASTD Press: Ashley McDonald
Community of Practice Manager, Learning Technologies: Justin Brusino
Editorial Assistant: Ashley Slade
Text and Cover Design: Marisa Kelly

Printed by Versa Press, East Peoria, IL, www.versapress.com

Contents

Foreword

Cindy Huggett grabbed my attention the first time I saw her present at an international conference for the American Society for Training & Development (ASTD). She was presenting on webinars and made it look easy and engaging. I could tell a lot of preparation and experience had gone into her session.

Impressed with her techniques for making webinar instruction and learning interactive, I introduced myself after class. Since then, we've had many conversations and I appreciate the insight and skill she has in making virtual learning become more alive. Out of these conversations came a foundation of trust and respect, and that led us to collaborate on *SCORE for Webinars*, which will come out in early 2014.

Cindy is such a valuable asset to the training industry, and I really value the time I spend working with her. She is a tremendous sounding board for ideas and has provided so much valuable guidance for me as a trainer, an author, and a company CEO.

In *The Virtual Training Guidebook*, Cindy provides a comprehensive guide to live online learning in an easy-to-follow, step-by-step format. The book begins with simple definitions and ends with how to measure online training effectiveness as well as a discussion on future trends.

However, I feel this book is such an excellent resource because, while detailing her process for virtual training, Cindy stays true to the most important aspect—interaction and engagement in the learning process. Throughout her work, she emphasizes the need to facilitate instruction and ensure participants are actively engaged in their learning.

After reading this book, I believe you will feel more comfortable and confident in handling the technical and technological aspects of virtual training.

Becky Pike Pluth
CEO of The Bob Pike Group
Author of *Webinars with WOW Factor*

Acknowledgments

A special thanks to the many business and training professionals who willingly shared their advice and stories about their experience with virtual training: Becky Pike Pluth, Cheryl Scanlan, Dan Gallagher, Danielle Buscher, Darlene Christopher, David Smith, Erin Laughlin, Jeff Robinson, Jennifer Newton, Jill Kennedy, Jim Wilcox, John Hall, Justin Patton, Kassy LaBorie, Ken Hubbell, Lisa Brodeth Carrick, Lorna Matty, Lucy Brown, Matt Murdoch, Peggy Page, Stephan Girard, Tara Welsh, Tracy Stanfield, Treion Muller, Trish Carr, and Wendy Gates Corbett, along with a few who chose to remain anonymous (you know who you are!). I am grateful to each one of them for their willingness to offer wisdom and their lessons learned. Their contributions have enriched this book. Thank you.

I'm also extremely grateful to Wendy Gates Corbett for all of the time and effort she spent reading early versions of the manuscript and for sharing her thoughts and suggestions on the content. Her insights were invaluable and made this book much better than it would have been otherwise.

Thank you also to Justin Brusino and Ashley McDonald at ASTD Press for their enormous patience during the lengthy book writing process. Their encouragement and advice carried this book through from concept to completion.

Finally, I dedicate this book to my best friend and husband, Bobby Huggett, who endured hearing me type on the keyboard for hours on end over many nights and weekends. Without his love and support this book would never have been written.

Cindy Huggett
Psalm 115:1
October 2013

Chapter ① Introduction

Join me online! Attend a free webinar! It's time to meet virtually! Invitation to a complimentary webcast! Your virtual lessons are now available!

These are the messages popping up in email inboxes everywhere. You have probably already seen at least one of these invitations in the past 24 hours. A review of my own recent email history reveals no less than 32 requests for online events in the past two weeks alone. To be fair, I'm sure I have a higher amount than the average person simply because of my work in virtual training. However, if you are like most, you have seen more and more of these types of messages in your daily routine.

Live online events have become a regular occurrence in today's business environment. Given the proliferation of today's technology tools, it's just as easy to video chat with someone across the globe as it is to talk with someone across the hallway. As society moves online, so does training.

Recent research backs up these anecdotal observations. According to the 2012 ASTD *State of the Industry* report, technology-based methods account for 37.3 percent of all learning delivery in organizations. Perhaps more significant for our purposes, the use of virtual training (defined as "instructor-led online learning") showed a 30 percent increase from 2010 to 2011 when it jumped from 6.7 percent to 8.8 percent of the overall mix (ASTD, 2012).

These numbers may not seem like much, but given that ASTD estimates $156.2 billion spent on learning and development in 2011, and employees averaged 31 overall hours of formal instruction, the amount of time and money spent on virtual training is significant. Significant enough to warrant attention.

Similar trends exist in higher education. The 2012 *Survey of Online Learning* conducted by the Babson Survey Research Group reveals that the number of college students taking at least one online course has surpassed 6.7 million. And 32 percent of higher education students now take at least one course online (Landry, 2012). While this book will not focus on education in the university setting, it's worth noting those trends; these college students will quickly become part of the workforce and will bring their online learning expectations and experiences with them.

So who is moving to the online classroom? Almost everyone is—and you can too!

Effectiveness of Virtual Training

Even though the use of online learning is expanding, many people are skeptical about virtual training for one reason or another. They may believe that it cannot replace in-person training under any circumstances. Or they don't trust that technology is reliable enough for meaningful online interaction.

Maybe you share this perception because of your own experience with poorly delivered online sessions. You might have experienced technical glitches during a virtual meeting, or listened to a boring online presenter drone on and on about an uninteresting topic. You are not alone! Many of us, myself included, have experienced these awful sessions.

It's been said that "only one in five people consider their company to be very effective at virtual training" (Mina, 2012). And passive webinars are notorious for encouraging participant multitasking—checking email and eating lunch while listening to someone else speak and click through a series of slides. But it doesn't have to be this way. Virtual training can be an effective method of learning and behavior change—if it's done well.

Numerous studies have shown that there is "no significant difference" in learning between online and face-to-face classes when all other factors are equal (Baker, 2010). A meta-analysis released in 2009 by the U.S. Department of Education found that "students who took all or part of their instruction online performed better, on average, than those taking the same course throughout face-to-face instruction" (Jaschik, 2009). More recently, 77 percent of academic leaders rate the learning outcomes in online education as the same or superior to those in face-to-face (Babson, 2012). While none of these research reports advocate the replacement of face-to-face learning experiences, or give credence to every type of online event, they open the door to the potential effectiveness of the virtual classroom. The possibility of well-designed, well-delivered, well-executed virtual training exists.

Benefits of Virtual Training

Not only can virtual training be effective, it can also be beneficial. Consider the many benefits of using live online training as a learning methodology in an organization:

Cost savings: Virtual training lowers travel costs for both participants and facilitators. While virtual training is not free—there are many other costs involved—it can result in overall reduced dollars spent.

- According to a recent benchmark report by Towards Maturity, over 80 percent of organizations surveyed that use significant amounts of virtual training are reducing travel costs, and almost 80 percent are reducing their overall training costs (2011). This finding is not surprising at all, and is echoed by most organizations that use virtual training.

Time savings: Virtual training is typically delivered in shorter chunks of learning time. This means less time away from the office, which often equals increased productivity.

- When employees can stay at their desks to participate in training, they will undoubtedly be able to accomplish more in a day than they would if they had to leave their workspace and go to a training class.

- A recent survey by ON24, Inc. revealed that 83 percent of HR and training professionals cite "more convenient" when asked about the benefits of virtual training (*Chief Learning Officer*, 2012). It's more convenient for participants, and more convenient for organizations.

Location: Virtual training can be delivered almost anytime, almost anyplace. If someone has a computer and reliable Internet connection, he or she can participate in a live online learning event.

- In fact, according to market research firm IDC, over 37 percent of the global workforce will be mobile by the end of 2015 (Eddy, 2012). And ASTD's recent research study on mobile learning shares that over 85 percent of organizations supply mobile devices to at least part of their workforce (ASTD, 2012). As your organization's workforce goes virtual, so can your organization's training.

Reach: Virtual training expands the reach of learning to those who might not receive training. It also connects people who might not normally get to collaborate together in a virtual class.

- The world continues to shrink in size, as organizations expand their reach across international borders. Your employees may frequently interact with people from around the world. Virtual training allows you the opportunity to create community without borders. Anyone with internet access can attend virtual training. And you can now provide training to employee populations who were previously excluded due to time, space, or location issues.

- According to the Towards Maturity report, "increasing access to learning" was the number one stated benefit (Towards Maturity, 2011).

"The number one reason we use virtual training is that it enables me to provide equality of access to training for our international staff in a cost effective way. The second reason is that it allows for collaboration across disperse geographies."

—Lorna Matty, Learning and Development Manager, Crown Agents

Why This Book?

In most books, resources, and references about virtual training, engaging delivery is usually touted as the most important key to success. Yes, it is important. However, I believe that engaging delivery is only one of many indicators about the quality of a virtual training experience. Several other key components that can make or break the success of virtual training are often overlooked in the intense focus on good delivery.

The critical success factors to virtual training include:
- having an intentional training plan in place
- putting the right technology into place
- designing interactive sessions
- preparing facilitators for virtual delivery
- preparing participants for a new way of learning
- paying attention to the administrative details.

It seems that we are missing the mark if we do not take a holistic view of virtual training. All of these items must be addressed if virtual training is to be a success. Yet, as the saying goes, we can "miss the forest for the trees" when we focus in on only one part of the formula.

In addition, as I talk with designers and facilitators around the globe about the full scope of what it takes to be successful at virtual training, so often I hear "would you please tell that to so-and-so in my organization?" They have collectively been trying to tell their managers that they need more budget for technology, or more time to design an interactive class, or more assistance with the administration of the details surrounding virtual training. Or they are forced to put hundreds of people into a virtual classroom, or to "make do" with sub-par resources. Designers and facilitators want their managers to recognize any misperceptions or misunderstandings about virtual training. More importantly, they want to have successful virtual training.

That's the goal of this book—to help organizations design, deliver, and implement excellent virtual training, as well as to take a complete look at all of the components needed to do virtual training well. And to help you ensure that your live online training is a good learning experience for participants. This book will help you do that.

This book is targeted to a wide audience—anyone who is involved with virtual training, from instructional designers to facilitating trainers to learning coordinators. Everyone who makes decisions about virtual training should know what it truly takes to deliver it well.

Format of the Book

This book addresses each of the critical success factors for virtual training—from conception to delivery to evaluation. It will take both the big-picture view of large virtual training implementations as well as a detailed view of single event virtual classes. It will look at what it takes to be successful when you first get started with virtual training, which is the soaring 50,000-foot view from above. And it will also address how to create effective individual virtual events, from the up-close 500-foot level.

Whether you are planning a large-scale virtual training rollout or want to hold just a single online class, you will find benefit from both views. And if you are still trying to decide if virtual training is right for you and your organization, then this book will help you learn what it takes to do it right.

In addition, throughout the book, you'll hear from trainers, designers, and organizations who have been down this journey. They'll share their experience and lessons learned. I think you will enjoy hearing their point of view, their tips, and their advice. I'll share from my own experience as well. Together we will paint a picture of successful virtual training.

Organization of the Chapters

The book is outlined as follows:

- **Chapter 2: Get Ready**—We will begin by helping you prepare your organization for virtual training, with a four-step process that leads to a successful launch. This chapter will look at the many definitions of virtual training, consider who should be involved in a virtual training rollout, and discuss how to build a business plan for virtual training in your organization.

- **Chapter 3: Select Technology**—This chapter outlines the types of technology needed for successful virtual training implementations. We'll consider hardware, software, and other technology needed. We'll also look at how to work with IT departments on selecting technology and how to partner with vendors.

- **Chapter 4: Design Content**—This chapter will provide an overview of best practice virtual training design principles, teach you a three-step design process, and give tips for converting traditional face-to-face courses to the online classroom. We will also review techniques to create facilitator and participant materials.

- **Chapter 5: Prepare Facilitators and Producers**—This chapter will define the roles needed for successful virtual delivery: facilitators and producers. We'll look at selection criteria for these roles, and show how to prepare them for delivering online. We'll also cover the art of online facilitation and delivery, which includes many tips and suggestions for creating an engaging learning environment.

- **Chapter 6: Prepare Participants**—An often overlooked component in virtual training success are the participants. It's a new way for them to learn! This chapter will provide tips and ideas for helping them adjust to the virtual classroom. We'll explore three techniques you can use to set them up for success.

- **Chapter 7: Create Success Through Logistics**—Details, details, details—it's all in the details! This chapter will focus on the administrative support and coordination needed to make virtual training a success. You'll learn the pre-event logistics to consider, day of event preparation, and post-event logistics such as assignments, surveys, and evaluations.

- **Chapter 8: Special Considerations: Global Issues, Evaluation Metrics, and Future Trends**—As we wrap up our discussion on virtual training, we will examine some special considerations. We'll focus on the unique considerations for global virtual training rollouts and cultural adaptations for virtual training: design, delivery, and logistics. We'll review how to evaluate success of your virtual training in your organization. And last, we will discuss some trends that are likely to have an impact on the future on virtual training.

Throughout the book, you'll also find many ready-to-use checklists and worksheets, which are also available for download from my website. Please visit www.cindyhuggett.com.

Let's begin!

Chapter ② Get Ready

In this chapter, you will learn four things you should do to get ready for a virtual training implementation:

- Ask yourself, "What's your end goal?"
- Define virtual training for your organization.
- Get the right people involved.
- Build an implementation plan.

Whether you want to have an extensive virtual training course curriculum that will require months of planning or only want to have one single online session, an implementation plan will help you get ready to use virtual training in your organization.

The first task in any implementation is to plan for success. As well-known author Stephen Covey once wrote, "Begin with the end in mind" (1989). The same thought is true for a virtual training implementation. Begin by thinking about the end goal.

Discover Your End Goal

The planning journey will start with your first step, which should be to ask yourself questions such as: What's our goal for this training program? What are we trying to accomplish? What do we want to be different as a result of it? Do we need participants to be more knowledgeable about a topic? Do we want them to behave differently? Take action on something? How will our organization change or improve as a result? What's the best way to achieve these goals? How specifically would *virtual* training help achieve these outcomes?

By answering these questions, you define your vision of virtual training success. You determine the purpose of your initiative and articulate your desired end result. By intentionally setting goals, you can increase your likelihood of achieving them. These questions can also help you determine if virtual training is the appropriate solution for your situation. Virtual training is not the answer just because everyone else is doing it or because it's a shiny object that captures your passing interest.

It may surprise you to hear that virtual training may not be the right solution for your organization. If by answering these questions, you realize that you're implementing virtual training just because you have heard it's a cheaper alternative to traditional training, or just because your employees are dispersed throughout the globe, or just because a competitor is doing it, then those are not the right reasons. All of these might be *contributing* factors to your reasons for wanting to implement virtual training. But the best reason to implement virtual training is that it will be the best solution to meet your organization's needs.

When done well, virtual training can transfer knowledge, increase productivity, help you gain competitive advantage, and positively affect business results. Virtual training can help you reach a global audience. It can reduce travel costs for training budgets. It can create opportunities for dispersed learners to interact with each other and a facilitator. And it can help provide training to participants who may otherwise not have access to instructor-led learning.

The point is that you should be clear about the reasons for using virtual training implementation. By beginning with the end, you can define what success will look like for your organization.

"Be really intentional about choosing {virtual training} as a modality. You both gain and give up. We've never promised that virtual training is the same learning experience as face-to-face training, but with a team located in cities around the world it's the most efficient way to deliver a consistent learning experience."

**—Dan Gallagher, Vice President of Learning at Comcast;
and author, *The Self-Aware Leader* (ASTD, 2012)**

Let's say, for example, your organization decides to decrease administrative costs worldwide by switching to a new online expense reporting system. End users need to learn how to use this new system in order for the costs savings to be realized. After looking at travel costs, participant locations, and trainer time, you determine that live online sessions will be the best way to both demonstrate and answer questions about the new features. You realize that virtual training will help you reach your geographically dispersed audience. And you believe the software skills content is suited to a virtual method.

So you might define the goals and objectives for this initiative by factoring in the organization's aim to decrease administrative costs and determining what end users specifically need to know and do with the new system features. These goals will help you define the learning objectives. But more importantly, they will help you design and deliver the appropriate type of virtual training for this initiative.

What type of virtual training will you deliver? That takes us to the next step in getting ready.

Define Virtual Training

One of the other most important things to do near the start of your journey is to define what your organization means by "virtual training."

Virtual training conjures up a myriad of definitions. While it probably means only one thing to you, it is certain to have a different meaning to someone else. You might think virtual training is any type of online course, while the person sitting next to you thinks virtual training is self-paced asynchronous learning. And the person down the hall might think virtual training is a webcast that has one presenter and hundreds of audience participants. Due to these disparate definitions, it makes sense to start by defining what you and your organization will mean when you say "virtual training."

No one is to blame that we have so many meanings of virtual training. If you look to how we use the term *virtual* in everyday life, the same pattern emerges. We talk about virtual reality, virtual teams, virtual wallets, virtual meetings, and virtual presentations, just to name a few. A cursory web search of the word "virtual" turns up over 1.2 billion hits. The lexicon of virtual training follows suit.

So what is virtual training? The definition I typically use is:

a highly interactive synchronous online instructor-led training class, with defined learning objectives, with participants who are individually connected from geographically dispersed locations, using a web-based classroom platform.

We'll peel apart that definition in a moment, but first, let's talk about what else virtual training could be.

To some, virtual training is any type of training delivered online. This definition would include asynchronous self-paced e-learning, as well as synchronous online classes. In this case, virtual training is considered to be synonymous with online learning. If it happens on the web, either alone or together with another person, then it would fit into their definition.

To others, virtual training encompasses any type of knowledge transfer that happens to be in an online environment. This definition includes webcasts, webinars, and online presentations. If any type of information is shared using a web conferencing platform, then it might be considered virtual training.

And still to others, virtual training refers to video conferencing or any type of telecommunication. A group of learners could be huddled together in a conference room in Pittsburgh, Pennsylvania, while another group could be together in Seattle, Washington, and a third group could be in Paris, France. They could be using their company's official video camera setup installed in each room, or a more informal online video sharing software. Just because participants are dispersed in multiple locations, some would consider this style of video conferencing to be virtual training.

The list of examples could go on. There are as many definitions of virtual training as there are types of training classes—**which is why you need to establish up front what you mean by virtual training, and get everyone involved on the same page.**

You might decide to use more than one type of virtual training in your organization. In fact, you probably will. Yet for each session, you should define exactly what your goal will be, and what method (that is, type of virtual training) you will use to get there.

I can't stress enough: Set the appropriate expectations with everyone involved. Be intentional about your goals for each virtual session and ensure that everyone is aware of those intentions. The success of your virtual training implementation will depend upon it.

"It's really important to call things by the right name and set those expectations. What you call something really influences the design and sets the stakeholders expectations."

—Peggy Page, Design Group Manager, TD Bank

Let's return to dissecting my definition of virtual training. It's one of the most common descriptions used. To remind you, the definition is: *a highly interactive synchronous online instructor-led training class, with defined learning objectives, with participants who are individually connected from geographically dispersed locations, using a web-based classroom platform.*

In other words, virtual training is (or has):

- *Highly interactive*—participants engage frequently, at least every few minutes, with the facilitator, with the learning content, and with the virtual classroom tools.

- *Synchronous*—participants meet together at the same time. Sometimes referred to as "live" or in the case of virtual training, live online.

- *Instructor-led*—facilitated by a professional trainer or instructor.

- *Defined learning objectives*—clearly stated performance expectations that learners will be able to achieve as a result of actively participating in the session.

- *Geographically dispersed participants*—learners are distributed and apart from one another. Moreover, each participant joins from his own device and has his own audio/telephone connection.

- *Web-based classroom platform*—a software program used for training that allows for online screen and file sharing, and has participant interaction tools such as polling, chatting, and annotating.

So a typical virtual training class might meet on a Thursday at 10 a.m., last 90 minutes, and have 18 participants from various locations around the country. The group would meet online using a synchronous tool, such as Adobe Connect or Citrix GoToTraining. The class would be led by a facilitator, and would result in the participants learning a new skill that could be immediately applied to their jobs.

Of course, your virtual training might not look like the one described above. You might have an alternate set of standards for timing, or number of participants, or even the learning outcomes. What's most important is that you define what your organization means by virtual training, and that everyone involved is on the same page.

Other Types of Live Online Sessions

Since so many of the tips found in this book can be applied to the various types of synchronous online sessions, let's also expand upon those common definitions.

What Does a Virtual Training Class Look Like?

In case you are brand new to virtual training, here is an illustration, adapted from my first book *Virtual Training Basics*.

Michelle is a trainer for a large telecommunications company. She's located in Cincinnati, Ohio and will be facilitating a 60-minute virtual class on Thursday morning at 11 a.m. Eastern time. About a week prior to the training date, she sends an email message with directions and logistics to her participants. About an hour prior to the start time, she sits at her office desk, logs into the virtual classroom software, and gets ready for the event. She uploads slides, opens the first polling question, and prepares the virtual whiteboard. She completes all of her pre-class preparation and waits for everyone to arrive.

Around 10:50 a.m. Eastern time on Thursday, the participants start entering the classroom. They do this from the comfort of their own respective offices: sitting at their own desks, opening up their Internet browsers, and clicking on the link from Michelle's email message.

One participant—Moira—is in her office in Dallas, Texas. She clicks on the link and goes straight to the login page. She types in her name and email address, and waits for the classroom software to load on her screen. Once connected, she sees the conference call number on screen, picks up her phone, and dials in, using her unique attendee ID displayed on screen. Moira hears Michelle's voice on the line, and says hello to greet her. The other participants follow the same steps to join the class.

The participants are able to see what Michelle has prepared for them on the screen. They see the names of the other attendees, the slides, a chat window, and the first polling question.

The participants communicate with each other verbally and online through frequent activities such as typing in the chat window, responding to polls, and writing on the whiteboard. At one point, Michelle assigns the participants into virtual breakout groups, and Moira is able to talk privately with her class partner Julie. They practice one of the new skills before returning to the large group for a debrief discussion.

By 12 p.m., class finishes, and Michelle asks everyone to complete a follow-up assignment to apply what they've just learned.

Webcast

A webcast primarily disseminates information from a speaker to a large audience. A speaker uses slides to present and share information. Sometimes a webcast includes multiple speakers or a panel of experts. And usually a webcast has a large audience, anywhere from a few dozen to a few thousand attendees.

A webcast is solely one-way communication from a presenter to attendees. Think about a traditional television newscast—with a news anchor reading from a script, using visual aids to illustrate stories, and interacting with other news presenters. A traditional newscast has little to no interaction with the audience, which is also true of a webcast.

If your organization were to pull a large audience together for a scripted town hall meeting, with presentations on the company strategy and only a short time for Q&A at the end, then this type of meeting—if held online—could be called a webcast.

Webinar

In its traditional definition, a webinar is an online seminar. Like a webcast, a webinar is also primarily one-way communication from a presenter to attendees. However, webinars often employ interactive techniques such as polling, chatting, or whiteboard annotating. If you think about how television newscasts have evolved over time, many modern news programs now incorporate audience interaction through social media and other techniques. For example, a reporter might respond to viewers' on-air questions or invite listeners to vote online and then report on the collected results.

It's the same with a webinar. The information shared is mostly one-way from speaker to audience. The speaker(s) use slides to present, while periodically involving attendees through polls and other brief interactions. While some webinars can be highly interactive, most are not.

You might think of a webinar like a university class, with an expert professor behind a podium and hundreds of students sitting in an auditorium. The class will have some interactivity through questions-and-answers, assignments, and quizzes. But the large class size limits the type and frequency of interaction available. If your organization's human resources department decided to hold informational sessions about a new company travel portal, and throughout the event they offered several opportunities for discussion and dialog, then this type of session—if held online—could be called a webinar.

Attend a Free Webinar!

A popular current trend is a specialized online session: the marketing webinar. Organizations use these marketing events to share information about their products and services to hundreds or even thousands of people. Organizations contract with thought leaders who speak on a subject, and invite everyone in their target market to this free event.

Attendees register for a session so they can hear from the expert speaker. Organizations use this registration data so they can capture interest and follow up with participants. At some point during the session, a sponsor's commercial is usually shared with attendees.

The positive trade-off is obvious—attendees learn something for free, while organizations capture valuable marketing data, and sponsors generate advertising.

The term *webinar* is so popular that many people believe it is synonymous with virtual training. It's increasingly common for organizations to call their virtual training sessions a webinar. Many popular speakers, authors, and trainers interchange the word webinar for virtual training. I've even done it myself on numerous occasions.

The intent behind calling virtual training a webinar is good—yet the effect can potentially create challenges for several reasons. First, participants who have attended passive webinars may expect to do the same in a virtual training class named a webinar. Second, presenters may assume the session should be lecture-based, and design and deliver the session accordingly. Third, administrators may unknowingly set up the event using a meeting platform instead of a training platform, which can affect the available features. When these expectations are mismatched—your intent is an interactive virtual training class but the result is a passive presentation—then there is higher risk for failure. Therefore, if you choose to call your sessions a webinar, as many organizations do, be prepared to climb any extra communication hurdles that may be required for success.

Webcast, Webinar, or Virtual Training?

The first main difference between a webcast, a webinar, and a virtual training class is the amount of participant interactivity in each one. Webcasts typically have the least amount of interaction, followed by webinars, then virtual training classes. The second main difference is the number of participants. Webcasts tend to be the largest, then webinars, followed by virtual training classes. There is not a simple black-and-white calculation that will tell you which is which; instead it's more like shades of grey on a continuum.

Video Conference

When participants are huddled together in a conference room using a video camera and viewing a screen that shows other groups huddled around other conference tables with the same setup, it would be called a video conference. Some would call it a virtual meeting. If this setup is used for learning, then it could be called remote training or distance learning.

Video conferencing systems used to be found only in sophisticated technology-enriched office meeting rooms; however, with new technologies and decreased costs, it's becoming more common for this same setup to substitute for virtual training.

If participants are together, and can see each other via video conference, then a trainer could join in and with the right design, facilitate a training class. It's synchronous, online, instructor-led, and has geographically dispersed participants. If you replace the video camera with a web conferencing platform then some would call it virtual training. But unfortunately, that's where defining this type of setup as virtual training can become confusing.

Most web conferencing platforms are designed for one person to use one computer. When a group of participants are sharing the same connection to a virtual training class, they have to combine their responses when responding to a poll, and take turns typing in the chat window. It's a different experience than each person connecting on their own.

The extra challenge is when you try to combine virtual training (one person with one computer) with video conferencing (groups sharing one connection in a conference room). This setup creates stress on the design because activities have to be designed in multiple ways for them to work. Single participants feel even more alone when they hear a room full of active learners, and the grouped together learners usually miss out on the platform's interactive features since they are not touching the keyboard.

If video conferencing is your definition of virtual training, then design, deliver, and implement for that type of training. It's not a good idea to mix and match the two methods in the same class.

"The worst mistake I have seen is treating a virtual webinar/training just like a meeting."

—Jill Kennedy, Learning & Development Specialist, Ally Financial

---

Blended Learning

When multiple delivery methods, including virtual events, are thoughtfully combined together into a training curriculum, the result is blended learning. Allison Rossett and Rebecca Vaughan Frazee define blended learning this way: "Blended learning integrates seemingly opposite approaches, such as formal and informal learning, face-to-face and online experiences, directed paths and reliance on self-direction, and digital references and collegial connections, in order to achieve individual and organizational goals" (Rosett and Frazee, 2006).

It's typical to find a combination of asynchronous self-paced activities and synchronous live instructor-led events in blended learning. For example, a learner in a blended interpersonal skills curriculum might receive instructions to complete a self-paced assignment, then attend two live virtual training events with another self-paced assignment in-between. Each of these components in the blended learning program is an important piece to the overall learning outcome. Learners need to complete all components to realize full results.

Blended learning is mentioned in this book because it's so common to find live online virtual training events as a significant component of a blended learning curriculum. You can apply the common phrase—*learning is a process, not an event*—by including virtual training in a blend. Stringing together multiple virtual events in a series allows for more flexible learning implementations. Instead of a single six-hour training session, the curriculum could be four 90-minute sessions spread out over time. It's also an opportunity for participants to learn something on their own and then meet together with a facilitator and other learners for skill practice.

For example, last year I designed a blended communication skills training program for one of my clients. The participants began by attending a virtual kickoff session to meet one another and learn about what to expect in the curriculum. They also received a short, self-paced assignment to help prepare themselves for the learning topics. Two weeks later, they met for an in-person workshop to learn and practice fundamental skills, again receiving an assignment at the end. Over the next four weeks, the participants met for two virtual training classes with application assignments in-between. The entire blended curriculum was approximately 24 hours of training time (including the assignments), and each component contributed to the learning outcomes.

What About a MOOC?

MOOC stands for "massive open online course." A MOOC is typically offered by colleges and universities as a way to open up education to all. Anyone with an Internet connection can sign up for a MOOC and participate in an online class, alongside traditional university students.

While MOOCs are currently popular, they are largely asynchronous, blended learning curriculums. Only if the MOOC instructor offered an interactive, live online segment would that piece of the course fall under our definition of virtual training.

Our Definition of Virtual Training

From this point forward, this book will refer to virtual training using my definition expressed above: *a highly interactive synchronous online instructor-led training class, with defined learning objectives, with participants who are individually connected from geographically dispersed locations, using a web-based classroom platform.* However, regardless of what your organization implements—virtual training, webcasts, webinars, video conferencing, or blended learning—the general principles outlined in this book will help you have a more successful online initiative.

Frequently Asked Questions About Virtual Training

Q: How long should a live online session be?

A: Virtual training classes tend to be shorter than their in-person classroom counterparts. A typical virtual session is 60 to 120 minutes in length. If you have more content than that length of time allows, consider chunking the content into smaller parts. It would be better to have three 90-minute virtual classes than to have a 4.5 hour continuous session. However, if you need to have a lengthy virtual class, be sure to take regular breaks throughout! We'll talk more about virtual class design in chapter 4.

Q: What about asynchronous e-learning? Isn't that considered virtual training?

A: In the sense that self-paced asynchronous e-learning can occur online, then some might consider it to be virtual training. However, it's most common to distinguish virtual training as synchronous, or live online, training. So this book follows that conventional format.

Get the Right People Involved

Once you have set forth your goals for virtual training and defined what you mean by it, get the right people involved with your virtual training initiative. Successful virtual training depends upon many parts of an organization. So getting the right people involved from the start will increase your chances of success.

There are at least three reasons for getting the right people involved at the start of your virtual training initiative. First, to gain their support. Second, to gain their input. Third, to make use of their available resources—both tangible (hardware, technology, funding) and intangible (wisdom, knowledge, experience).

How do you know who to include in these initial conversations? In smaller organizations, the answer will probably be obvious. In larger organizations, the answer will mean doing your homework and finding out who the stakeholders are for each part of your virtual training initiative. Either way, it's better to invite more input than needed than to keep the information to yourself and potentially miss a key player.

"My advice? Involve everyone in the organization up front. Different teams have different roles to play in the virtual training initiative."

—**Danielle Buscher, Director of Global Learning, Marriott International**

The typical roles involved with a virtual training rollout are listed below. Note that these may not be job titles, per se, but are job functions that carry out responsibilities that affect the success of virtual training. Also, in some organizations, one person may play more than one role. For example, the instructor who delivers virtual training may also have been the person who designs it. Or the facilitator and the administrator might be the same person. The smaller the organization, the more likely it is to have one person spanning multiple roles. And on the flip side, there may be more than one person for each function, such as an IT representative for each location.

- **Content owners:** Sometimes referred to as a subject matter expert (SME), this person has deep knowledge of the training topic. They might be an employee in the field, or a manager with responsibility for the subject matter. They can help design the training and ensure topic relevancy.

- **Designers:** Instructional designers create the training. This role might include graphic designers as well as workplace learning professionals who specialize in adult learning methodologies and instructional technology.

- **Facilitators:** Also called trainers or instructors, this is the person in "front" of the class who delivers the virtual training sessions.

- **Producers:** These are the technical experts who assist a facilitator during a live online session. Some producers specialize in technology-only assistance (working with participants who need help connecting), while other producers co-facilitate sessions along with the trainer. In some cases, a producer may be called a host or session moderator.

- **Coordinators:** As the administrative person who handles logistical details of virtual training events, this person might administer the organization's LMS (learning management system), as well as communicate with participants before and after an event.

- **Technicians:** Usually called IT (information technology) or IS (information services), this role owns the technology—both hardware and software—needed for virtual training success.

- **Participants:** They are otherwise known as learners or in some cases, program attendees. Since they are the "customer" or "end user" of the virtual training initiative, consider including a representative sample in your initial planning stages.

- **Managers:** As the participants' managers, they need to support the full participation of their employees. This group's buy-in is critical to success because they will allow participants time to attend training, as well as reinforce the skills learned.

- **Resource Owners:** These stakeholders control resources needed for creating, designing, delivering, and implementing virtual training. This group could be training management, who directs the training function and its associated resources. Or it could be general management who controls budget and other needed resources.

- **Executive Sponsor:** The senior executive is the individual who can support and champion the virtual training initiative at the highest levels of the organization.

We will explore many of these roles in more detail in other places in this book. For now, it's most important to realize that each one can contribute to the success of your virtual training initiative. Involve them in the earliest stages.

"Our project team included human resources, IT, training design and development, and all of the subject matter experts for each part of the curriculum."

—Erin Laughlin, Senior Director Global Learning Delivery,
Marriott International

Once you have invited the right people to the table for discussion, have an open dialogue with each about what it will take for success from their perspective. This dialogue could be one-on-one conversations, or it could be a cross-functional project team discussion. The communication format is not as important as actually having communication with key players.

Which Comes First?

Should you start with determining your goals and defining what you mean by virtual training, and then get the right people involved? Or should you get the right people involved first, so that they can help you establish goals and define virtual training? The answer...it depends. There's not a right or wrong answer. What's most important is that you actually do all of these things.

In your communication with these stakeholders, start by sharing the answers you already uncovered: what is the end goal of this initiative and how you define virtual training. Depending on the exact timing of these conversations and your organization's unique situation, you might even gain their input to these questions.

After sharing the overarching goals, select the appropriate discussion questions from this list below:

❍ What suggestions or recommendations do you have?

❍ What questions or concerns do you have?

❍ From your view, what will it take to be successful?

❍ What resources do you need for your part of the initiative? What resources can you contribute?

❍ Who else should be involved with this initiative?

❍ Will I have your support?

If you form a cross-functional team, follow standard project management processes for your implementation. Hold a kickoff meeting, create a project charter, and clearly define each person's role in the project.

Build a Plan

The fourth step to getting ready is to build an implementation plan. It's possible that when you gather stakeholders to discuss the plan, you may need to step back and start with a business case—just to gain support for the initiative. However, if you are fortunate enough to already have financial and resource support, that's fantastic! You could still benefit from working through the suggestions in this step even without needing to follow through on them, to help crystallize your training implementation plans. On the other hand, if you do need to build a business case—to gain support for the program or to negotiate for resources—use the momentum created so far to move forward with your proposal.

If you need to build a business case for virtual training, start with your objectives. Articulate who will benefit from the initiative, and exactly how they will benefit. Spell out the anticipated positive impact to the organization. Identify both the costs and the potential return-on-investment.

A typical business case includes the following items:

- overview of the business problem to solve

- recommended solution to the problem

- benefits of the recommended solution

- resources needed, including cost and financial details

- expected results to be realized.

The business case for virtual training should be presented to whoever controls resources needed and has the authority to share those resources. All or some of the business case might also be presented to key stakeholders to help them see the benefits of virtual training.

Wendy Gates Corbett, a global training director, created a business case to establish virtual training as a method to help her company's global customer base learn about their software products. Her proposal to her executive team included facts about the potential for virtual training, suggested solutions for realizing that potential, and the resources they would need. She established the benefits and outlined the expected return on their investment. Spelling out these details gave her the momentum and approval needed to launch the plan for virtual training.

Building a Business Case at the World Bank Group

To build the business case for virtual training at the World Bank Group, Learning Officer Darlene Christopher wisely connected virtual training to an important corporate initiative. At that time, her organization was looking to reduce its carbon footprint to create a more sustainable environment. Darlene calculated the carbon emissions savings that would be realized by conducting virtual training instead of in-person training. She converted the emissions savings into tangible results (for example, "By hosting one virtual session we will avoid 44 tons of carbon emissions, which is equivalent to recycling 13.8 tons of waste or growing 1024 trees for 10 years"). The excitement over the potential for virtual training literally grew out of this message, which was tied to helping the business achieve its goals.

Darlene's advice to others is to start small. Find a willing stakeholder or two within your organization who will support a simple virtual training initiative. Get an early win, and then think about what story you can tell from that experience. By starting small, you can get others interested and excited about the initiative, and then build traction from there. Think about what corporate initiative you could tie into for support, and how virtual training can help your organization achieve its goals.

Calculating the Costs of Virtual Training

You may be part of an organization that chooses virtual training to save costs. For example, travel budgets have been slashed and flying to deliver or attend in-person training is no longer allowed. In this case, a traditional business case is probably not needed because key stakeholders gave instructions to reduce funding as opposed to granting it.

What *is* needed in this scenario is a business case that explicitly outlines the true costs of effective virtual training. Since the expectation would be to reduce or even eliminate funding, you will need a solid business case to clearly illustrate the costs of implementing virtual training. Virtual training is perceived to be less expensive than traditional in-person training; however, that perception is not always reality.

Virtual training does reduce travel expenses when learners are able to stay at their desks instead of hop on a plane or drive to a training location. However, virtual training includes costs that did not exist for in-person training. These costs could include new telephone headsets for all participants, increased administrative fees for the additional logistics, significant conference calling charges, additional design time, and the cost of two facilitators (or a facilitator and a producer) for each virtual event.

Use the following chart to compare how your costs may change as a result of using virtual training:

Table 2-1 The Costs of Virtual Training

Costs	Increase or Decrease (as compared to traditional classroom training)
Virtual classroom software platform licenses	Increase
Integrated telephone/conference call subscription and per-event costs (if not using VoIP)	Increase
Computer hardware needs, such as hands-free telephone headsets for participants	Increase
Printing costs of classroom materials	Decrease
Printing costs for learners (who are often asked to print their own materials)	Increase
Two facilitators, or a facilitator and a producer, for each virtual event (See chapter 5 for more information about this item)	Increase
A second laptop for facilitators who should be logged into the platform twice (once as a presenter and once as a participant)	Increase
Training for staff (designers and facilitators) who need to learn the new virtual classroom software platform and how to design/deliver virtual training	Increase
Design and development time of the training curriculum[1]	Increase
Travel fees for both participants and facilitators	Decrease
Classroom materials that no longer need to be purchased (i.e., chart paper, markers, etc.)	Decrease
Productivity for participants who do not have to leave their desks to attend training in another location	Increase

---

1. According to research by Karl Kapp and Robin Defelice, it takes on average 43 hours of development time to create one hour of instructor-led training, and it takes approximately 49 hours of development time to create one hour of interactive virtual training. For more information, visit http://www.astd.org/Publications/Newsletters/Learning-Circuits/Learning-Circuits-Archives/2009/08/Time-to-Develop-One-Hour-of-Training.

"We took a two-day performance management course and converted it into a blended learning program. The new converted program included six virtual sessions along with self-paced assignments. This new solution created efficiency for learners; however, it increased the administrative work required for the trainer and the program manager. Don't assume that because you're saving on airfare that virtual training will be less expensive. While you save on learner expenses, you often increase your design, delivery, and administrative costs."

—Dan Gallagher, Vice President of Learning at Comcast; and author, *The Self-Aware Leader* (ASTD, 2012)

By fully considering the true costs of virtual training in your organization, you can 1) request appropriate funding in your business case, and 2) set yourself up for success in your initiative.

Creating an Implementation Plan

Once you have support and resources to move forward with virtual training, the next step is to create an implementation plan. This project plan will detail your strategy for rolling out virtual training in your organization. To create it, you'll need input from key stakeholders, as well as timelines and deliverables for each step of the process.

The complexity of your implementation plan will match the complexity of your project. The strategy and detail needed to establish a comprehensive virtual training curriculum will differ from the amount of detail needed to plan a one-time virtual class.

Regardless of the size of your virtual training initiative, a typical implementation plan will include considerations for design, delivery, and administration. We will explore each of these topics starting with the next chapter.

One Organization's Story

Way of Life Coaching, LLC based in Raleigh, North Carolina, offers an eight-month group coaching course called "Promised Land Living." Founder Cheryl Scanlan's vision was to expand the reach of this program beyond the local community. She wanted to make the curriculum available to anyone regardless of their geographic location.

After careful consideration of various options, Cheryl decided to convert the program to an all-virtual curriculum. Together with her team she started planning what it would take to make it happen. They worked together for months as they planned out the implementation strategy.

They:

- budgeted resources for the new delivery methodology
- redesigned the content for virtual delivery
- involved subject matter experts and stakeholders for advice and input
- researched and selected a virtual training platform
- created a marketing plan to communicate the new program format
- worked with participants and facilitators to help them get comfortable with virtual training.

Cheryl's advice to other organizations who are considering the move to virtual? "Get familiar with the virtual training platform, and how often the vendor makes updates to it. Be sure you test drive the platform after upgrades to make sure there are no surprises. I would also highly recommend that you have a producer for every virtual class so that you can be about the business of delivering your material. That made all the difference for us and our clients!"

In Summary: Key Points From Chapter 2

- Determine if virtual training is the right training solution for your organization.

- Define what you mean by virtual training and ensure everyone in your organization shares that same definition.

- Get the right people involved in your virtual training, as close to the project start time as possible.

- If needed, create a business case to secure enough resources for your virtual training plan.

Checklist 2-1 Is Virtual Training the Right Solution?

To help determine if virtual training is the correct solution to use for your organization, consider the following questions:

○ **Are the participants centrally located or dispersed?** If your organization is not going to save on travel expenses because everyone is in the same location, then consider sticking with in-person training. It may be just as fast for them to walk down the hallway to your training room as it would be for them to log in to a virtual classroom.

○ **What technology barriers affect success?** Participants need to have the appropriate technology available to them. The exact technology needed will vary depending upon the virtual software program used; however, a typical technology setup requires a high-speed Internet connection, a sound card and speakers to hear streaming media, and administrative privileges to install software. Our next chapter addresses technology factors.

○ **Do you have qualified trainers and producers to facilitate the virtual training event?** Classroom trainers need a new skill set to effectively deliver virtual training. They need to be comfortable with technology, able to multitask well, and know how to engage participants who they can't see. These skills come with training and practice; however, this trainer preparation time should be factored into the decision. In addition, a virtual training event will go much smoother with producer involved with the facilitation. The producer is a second person who assists the trainer with technology, troubleshooting, and running the virtual event. They help create a seamless experience for participants. We will consider trainer and producer qualifications in chapter 5.

○ **Will every participant have an appropriate learning environment?** Participants need to have their own individual computer connection and telephone line to attend the virtual event. They should be in a quiet area conducive to learning. If they are in an open space or cubicle environment, they will need headphones or another way to tune out external noise. Chapter 6 provides a comprehensive look at how to set up participants for effective online learning environments.

○ **Who will administer the logistical details for the training program?** The online environment creates a long list of logistics that need to be executed for a successful class. This includes creating the virtual classroom event(s) within the software's administrative tools, getting links and passwords to everyone who needs them, distributing handouts and other class materials to participants, and helping participants troubleshoot technical problems prior to class. Chapter 7 covers all of the administrative details that will be needed for your initiative.

○ **Do all participants speak the same language?** Virtual training can be an excellent way to provide training to an international population, as long as language barriers do not get in the way. Note that chapter 8 focuses on other global considerations.

Worksheet 2-1 Goal Setting

What's our goal for this training program? What specifically are we trying to accomplish?

_____

_____

What do we need participants to do as a result?
- ○ Be more knowledgeable about the topic?
- ○ Behave differently?
- ○ Take action on something?

_____

_____

How will our organization change or improve as a result?

_____

_____

What's the *best* way to achieve the above goals?

_____

_____

How specifically will *virtual* training help achieve these outcomes?

_____

_____

Chapter ③

Select Technology

In this chapter, you will learn how to select technology for your virtual training:

- Consider four factors: hardware, audio, software, and bandwidth.
- Partner with IT to select technology.
- Select technology vendors.

Technology is supposed to make our lives easier. It automates tasks, it speeds things up, and it helps us get things done. Unfortunately, there are times when it doesn't work as planned. And then we get frustrated. What's supposed to make life easier ends up making it more complicated.

For example, if you plan on writing a document and use word processing software to create it, you are saving time and effort because the software automates the typing and editing. It's much easier than years ago when you used a typewriter and correction tape. You can use the software's save command to store your document in a safe place and return to it at a later time. However, it's possible for things to go unexpectedly wrong. If it's not saved correctly, the document can be damaged, corrupted, or even lost. The technology that was supposed to be helpful ends up creating more challenges.

Or say, for instance, you rely on a smartphone maps application to guide you to a destination. You listen to its voice commands as it directs you from one turn to the next. It gets you to your location using the most efficient route. But if the maps application doesn't have accurate data, then it will lead you astray.

It's the same with the technology you use for virtual training. You want the technology to make your training easier, to help you save time, and to guide you to your learning destination. But you don't want it to interfere or get in the way. You just want it to do its job, seamlessly.

Many people have experienced—and you probably have too—technology challenges during virtual training classes. It's so common that many people actually associate virtual training with technology problems. But it doesn't have to be that way. You can have successful virtual training classes that run flawlessly and with ease. The technology should be unnoticed, just the means to the learning end. And for that to happen, it takes thoughtful planning, selecting, and implementing. When the technology is doing its job, it will work smoothly, do what it needs to do, and not interfere or get in the way. It shouldn't be a stumbling block. Instead, it should be the supporting scaffold for learning.

What makes virtual training possible is the technology. Even though it's the vehicle for virtual training, the technology shouldn't be the center of attention. That's because it's not the star of the show. The star is the learning—the participant's new skills or their behavior change. Technology stays behind the scenes, playing a supporting role.

So what kind of technology do you need for a successful virtual training rollout? And how do you ensure that the technology runs seamless and smooth? This chapter will answer those questions.

In general, there are four aspects of technology to consider for a virtual training implementation:

- hardware

- audio

- software

- Internet bandwidth.

Let's review the details of each one so that you can make appropriate selections for your virtual training technology.

Run, Don't Walk

Go get your contact in the IT department and read through this chapter together. Use this opportunity to discuss what technology you already have, what technology you need, and how to close the gap between those two.

Hardware

The obvious equipment each participant needs for virtual training success is a computer with a stable Internet connection. It's the computer that runs the software that allows the learning to happen. The hardware could be a laptop or a computer, of any make, model, or brand, provided that it meets the hardware requirements of the software platform you choose.

Most platform providers will inform you of the hardware requirements for their program. For example, you'll need X amount of memory, minimum Internet connection speed of Y, and enough hardware space for any necessary software downloads.

Sample Virtual Training Platform Hardware Specs

- 2 GHz or faster processor
- 500 MB RAM
- 20 MB free disk space
- Windows, Mac, or Linux Operating System
- Compatible Internet browser (such as Microsoft Internet Explorer, Mozilla Firefox, Apple Safari, or Google Chrome)
- Broadband Internet connection

Every person attached to the virtual training session needs to have his or her own computer connection. Remember, this book's definition of virtual training is not the same as remote training where a group of people are gathered around a conference room table passively watching on screen. Instead, in virtual training, each participant connects individually to the class.

In today's business environment, this point may seem like a no-brainer. Of course we like to think that everyone has a computer. But do they? There are plenty of industries and organizations that do not supply individual computers to their workforce, such as some retail employees, construction workers, or manufacturing operators.

If providing individual computers is not an option for your organization, then consider the following:

- What other business needs could be met by providing individual computers to your workforce? Is now the right time for this to happen? Could the individuals, and the organization, benefit as a result? If so, strive to make it happen.

- Is virtual training the best answer for your organization? It may not be. As discussed in the previous chapter, there are many reasons to use virtual training as a learning solution for your organization. However, there are times when it is not. If your workforce will not benefit from virtual training, or they are not able to take full advantage of this learning modality due to their physical locations or lack of equipment, then there may be a better option for their learning.

- Could participants "borrow" a computer from your organization's lending library? Should you establish a lending library for this purpose?

- Is there a shared space that could be set up or created for virtual learning? A "hotel style" office space that has an individual learning laboratory set up?

- Are mobile devices robust enough for your solution? If so, could those be provided to your participants? We will explore the unique usage of mobile devices for virtual training in the next section; for now, just consider the possibility.

Facilitator Hardware Requirements

You should also consider the hardware needed for facilitators. Most facilitators will need not just one, but two computers to effectively deliver virtual training. We'll dive deep into the facilitator role in chapter 5 and talk more about what exactly they do with both connections. For now, the essential reasons for two facilitator computers are as follows:

- So the facilitator can view the host or presenter login as well as the participant view. The facilitator needs to be able to discuss and explain exactly what the participant sees on their computer screens. It's also essential to see any and all nuances of the software that's unique to the participant view.

- So the facilitator has a backup computer to use in case of technology failure or other unexpected glitch. This is especially important if the facilitator is solo without a co-presenter or producer. (You will learn more about the importance of these roles in chapter 5.)

If your organization has a standard issue "one computer per person," it may be time to make an exception to that rule for virtual trainers. Many seasoned online facilitators find a way to use multiple computers per session—either by using their personal computer as well as their company computer during a virtual training session or by borrowing a second computer from someone who doesn't need it during that short timeframe.

If providing a second computer isn't possible, then perhaps a shared "training computer" could be used among facilitators. Or follow the footsteps of several organizations that have designated a virtual training room with computers already set up in it (similar to the hotel style office mentioned above for participants).

Cost Consideration

If the cost of a second computer for facilitators is an issue, think of it this way: Eliminating the cost of just one or two airplane tickets for a traveling trainer would cover the approximate cost of a basic computer.

In a similar vein, if your organization only allows one authenticated login per user, be sure to create a second account for the facilitator to use on the second computer. One of my clients created generic "trainer" network users (such as "Trainer One," "Trainer Two," "Trainer Three") so that facilitators could have multiple devices connected at once.

Mobile Devices

It may be possible to use mobile devices in lieu of a computer for virtual training. The proliferation of mobile technology use in the workplace, and the increased capability of software platforms that work with mobile devices, allows participants greater flexibility when connecting to a session.

At the time of this writing, mobile devices can be used to connect to many online meetings and virtual events. Most virtual classroom software platforms have apps that correlate to their online programs. Unfortunately, however, most of these apps currently have limited functionality as compared to the full computer version of the program.

For example, a participant connected to a session via mobile device may see a different view than everyone else. The mobile view might only show one area of the screen at a time, instead of the full view. A mobile participant may or may not be able to use the annotation tools in the same way as on the computer. He may not be able to answer poll questions. Each platform has differing feature limitations in their app versions.

Recently I co-facilitated a virtual class and many participants joined the session via a tablet device. The specific platform we used had a mobile app, which made connecting to the class easy. The participants were able to fully participate in the first few activities. But the trouble began when I opened the first multimedia clip. Only those connected by computer were able to watch the clip, and those who were connected via app just saw an error message that said "this feature is not supported." A little later in the session, we began a whiteboard activity. Those who were connected by computer used the text annotation tool to type on the screen. But those connected from their mobile device could only use the annotation drawing tools to freehand draw. They didn't have a text tool that allowed for typing on screen. While these two situations may seem like small limitations, they can make a big difference in the learning effectiveness. It's worth noting these challenges when considering the use of mobile devices for virtual training.

The limitations of mobile apps for virtual training are rapidly diminishing, and will most likely not be an issue at some point in the future. Mobile apps will update, software platforms will evolve, and features will become seamless between computer and mobile versions.

Another issue with mobile devices may be ensuring a stable Internet connection with enough bandwidth to handle the virtual class needs. Participants who use mobile devices will need to ensure they are in a place with reliable steady service, or they have a data plan capable of supporting the class connection needs. While using mobile devices for virtual training may be common in the future, for now, the limited functionality of mobile apps creates challenges.

If mobile devices will be used in your organization for virtual training, designers and facilitators will need to adapt activities to accommodate these users. Designers will need to be aware of all features and limitations and design the session accordingly. The result will most likely be less interaction and more presentation.

Audio

Telephony is a broad term referring to the overall audio connection and telephone equipment used for the verbal portion of a virtual training session. The audio connection allows for verbal communication—a key component of engaging virtual training. Through telephony, a learner can hear the facilitator and talk with fellow class participants.

There are two types of audio connections that can be used for virtual training sessions:

- conference call (either stand-alone or integrated with the virtual platform)

- Voice over Internet Protocol (VoIP).

If you choose a technology solution that uses conference calling, then each participant will need a reliable telephone connection and a headset for hands-free use. If you use VoIP, then each participant's computer will need to have a sound card, with either speakers and a microphone or a headset that combines these two.

Which audio connection type should you choose? It depends on the virtual platform software you'll use, the Internet bandwidth speeds available to participants, and your budget dollars. With conference calling, you have an extremely reliable audio connection via telephone. The sound quality should be crystal clear for everyone.

In a *stand-alone conference call,* the audio is not connected to the virtual classroom software. They are independent of each other. While this setup provides redundancy in case of technical failure, it may not allow for using breakout room features and other audio commands that are built into software.

Integrated conference calling means that the audio and visual components of the virtual class are connected behind the scenes. Everyone still uses their telephone to dial into the audio portion of the call; but the audio commands, such as mute/unmute, can be controlled from the classroom's web platform. Features that use audio, such as breakout rooms, are available to all. It's also easy to tell who is speaking at any given moment, provided the software includes this feature.

VoIP audio is most commonly used for webcasts and webinars, where the presenter is doing most of the talking. It's certainly possible to use VoIP connections for a virtual training class, if every participant has the appropriate hardware needed: a sound card, speakers, and microphone. These pieces can be separate, or combined as a mono or stereo headset that connects to the computer. When using VoIP, participants could to be able to speak freely and easily during class, or they may have to "request microphone rights" to speak one at a time.

One advantage of VoIP is there is typically no additional cost associated with the audio connection. You might consider it to be bundled audio with the software. Unfortunately, this is also the drawback of VoIP, because it takes extra Internet bandwidth space. In some cases, this extra space is enough to cause considerable quality issues and unclear sound connections.

Figure 3-1 Adobe Connect Audio Options

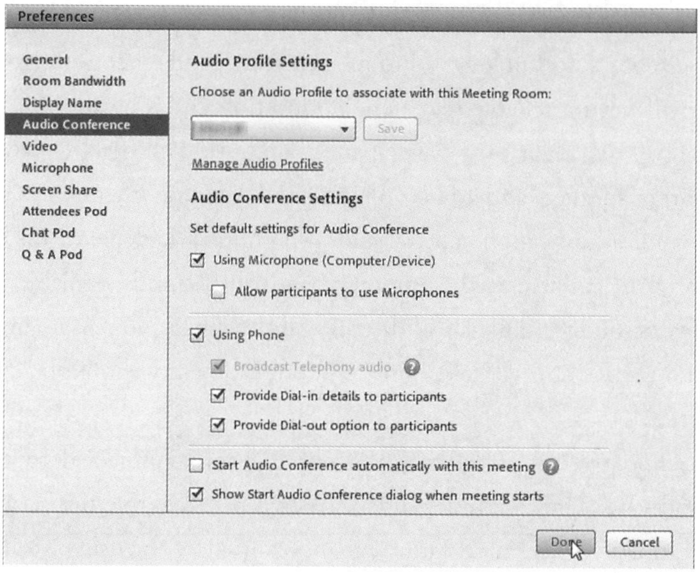

As with everything, while working with your hardware, software, and telephony, you will spend a considerable amount of time testing prior to any virtual training session. You will discover any of these glitches well in advance and be able to fix or work around them.

In addition, when using VoIP, the visual and audio are using the same connection. Therefore, if the Internet connection is lost for any reason, all communication will be lost at the same time. So if the facilitator unexpectedly loses connectivity during class, they would not be able to continue until they reconnected. If they had been using the telephone instead, then the facilitator could at least continue talking with participants and let them know what was happening while he reconnected.

Also, when considering your audio choice, be sure to factor telephony costs into your budget, especially if you will have long-distance and international callers. Standard conference calling rates typically apply.

One platform I use gives me the choice over whether or not a toll-free number is shared with participants. To keep costs down for this particular program, my client chooses to only offer the long-distance area code dialing option. In this case, participants bear the cost burden of the telephony.

Headsets

Without question, you should provide headsets for participants and facilitators. Imagine trying to cradle a phone on your shoulder for 60 to 90 minutes, while typing and frequently engaging in a class. It's not a pleasant image, nor a pleasant feeling. By investing in basic headsets you will enable your learners the chance to focus on the training and not on the pain they feel in their neck.

You also want to avoid the use of speaker phones, which can give off an echo, pick up extraneous noises, and generally does not sound good in a virtual classroom. Participants who use speakerphones may also distract their neighbors who sit nearby. Whether you use a conference call or VoIP for audio, participants should have a headset to fully participate in class.

One of my recent class participants mentioned that headsets have now become standard-issue equipment for all employees in their organization because they frequently use virtual training methods. The organization wanted to ensure that everyone was equipped appropriately.

Software

The most important software needed for a virtual training rollout is your virtual classroom platform. Sometimes it's called a web conferencing program, an online collaboration platform, or virtual meeting software. I typically refer to them as virtual classroom software programs or the virtual platform.

To select the best software for your virtual training rollout, you should:

- determine what features you need

- partner together with your IT department on decision making

- research vendors who offer solutions that match.

Determine What Features You Need

It is extremely important to familiarize yourself with the common features found in most programs. In fact, everyone who uses or interacts with this software should be familiar with its features and functionality. Administrators need to know the setup and behind-the-scenes operations. IT staff need to know how to install and troubleshoot the program. Designers need to understand how all the features work so that they can create engaging classes using the tools. Facilitators and producers need to be expert users. Participants need to feel comfortable with its use.

I'll help you get started by reviewing some basic features and functionalities of a virtual classroom platform. Please note that each platform has its own nuances and specific functionality for each item, and some platforms lack these features altogether. It will be important for you to research and uncover what's included with your selected platform.

By the way, if you're already an expert user, skip this section and catch up with us on the next step, partnering with IT.

Categories of Virtual Classroom Software Programs

Most virtual classroom software programs are part of a suite of products that offer various versions. For example, Cisco WebEx has Event Center, Meeting Center, Training Center, and Support Center. And there is Citrix GoToMeeting, GoToTraining, and GoToWebinar.

The most important decision you can make is which product version of the software you will use. Each variation of the platform has different features and functionality. While it's possible to use a vendor's meeting product for virtual training, it's often not the best alternative. It's also possible to use the webinar version of the software, which is again often not the best solution for virtual training.

To illustrate, a vendor's meeting product usually does not include breakout group functionality, which is a key feature used in many small group training sessions. And the webinar version usually does not include public chat, which means that participants can only communicate with the presenter and not each other during a session.

In most cases, you should select the training version of the software platform. It may be more expensive than the meeting version, but the additional training features offer a substantial advantage when creating and delivering highly interactive sessions.

Common Tools in a Virtual Classroom Software Program

Most virtual classroom software programs have similar features and functionality. The following list, adapted from my first book *Virtual Training Basics,* includes the tools most often used in virtual training (Huggett, 2010). Please note that this is not an exhaustive list of all features found in every platform, nor is it an endorsement for a particular platform. In selecting a platform, you should research and discover the nuances for each of these tools and how they specifically work in each program.

Sharing Documents

Sharing documents is one of the most commonly used features in a virtual class. The facilitator uploads a file into a viewing window and all participants can see it. When the trainer navigates through the document, moving from one page to another, the participants' screens follow along.

Almost all virtual training classes use document sharing to display slides. In addition, other documents, such as training manuals or pages from the class handout, can also be displayed.

Each platform has compatibility requirements for documents shared. Most programs can share Microsoft Office documents (Word, Excel, PowerPoint), plus Adobe Portable Document Format (PDF) files. Many can also share an audio or video media file, which means that prerecorded videos can be shown during a class. If you know you will need to share certain file types, check for file compatibility when considering your platform.

Some platforms have participant privilege settings that give the participants greater control over the shared documents. They may be able to draw on the document, or even move around the document independently. Or, they may be able to share their own documents for a group collaboration exercise.

Most classes include multiple shared documents. For example, one of my virtual training classes on coaching typically has at least five shared documents: a welcome slide deck with introductory material, the class slide deck that contains course content, an excerpt from the participant handout that we use in an activity, a video file that plays during class, and an audio music file that we listen to during a group exercise. I share each document in turn during the class.

Figure 3-2 Adobe Connect Share Pod

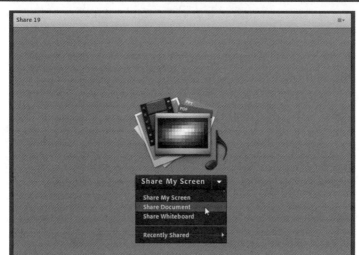

Chat

Chat enables communication between and among participants through real-time typed messages. Chat can be public so that everyone can see, or sent privately to one individual user. Chat allows for participant engagement during a training class. Participants can send feedback, ask questions, and make comments during the class. The chat window can be a running commentary for participant dialogue throughout the session. Chat can also be used during activities for participants to answer questions. It creates another way for participants to respond when questions are posed by the facilitator.

The chat window can also be useful for the trainer to pass messages along to the participants during activities. For example, during a breakout session, the trainer can use the chat window to give timing reminders (such as "three minutes remaining," or "it's time to begin round two").

Rules about private chat vary from program to program. In many cases, the facilitator can choose whether or not private chat is allowed, and if it is allowed, if participants can privately chat with the facilitator only, or also with each other.

Private chat could also be used to create a "paired" discussion opportunity in class. Similar to a classroom session where a trainer says "turn to the person sitting next to you and discuss your response to this question," a virtual class activity could direct participants to have a private chat. This is one of my personal favorite ways to use the chat feature because it involves every single participant in the dialogue.

Peggy Page, the Design Group Manager at TD Bank, also uses the chat feature extensively when designing virtual classes. Since some of her participants connect from a wide-open space (desks situated in the bank lobby), and they are not able to easily talk during a session without disturbing those around them, they use chat as the way to communicate. Peggy wouldn't call these events "virtual training" due to their limited interactivity, yet she has found a way via chat to keep participants' attention during short virtual sessions.

Figure 3-3 Adobe Connect Chat Pod

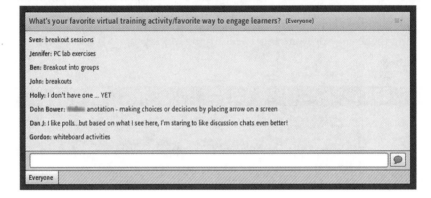

Annotate

Annotate

Annotation allows for real time drawing and typing on top of shared documents or a whiteboard. The exact annotation tools available vary from platform to platform. However most allow you to:

- highlight words or graphics
- draw lines and other shapes
- draw freehand with an electronic pencil or marker
- type text on the screen.

Most platforms have the ability to turn on or off the annotation rights for participants and facilitators. They also include varying degrees of erasers—some allow a person to erase only their own added content, while others have only an "erase all" command.

The annotation tools help keep the screen visually interesting when the facilitator "highlights" key words while speaking. When participants are able to draw or mark on the screen, it helps engage them into the learning content. A facilitator can ask learners to draw or type on screen in response to a question, or ask them to highlight something on screen that stands out to them.

For example, at the end of a class, it's a common practice to ask participants to share an insight they gained or an action they will take. Using the annotation tools, participants could write these items on screen for all to see. They could also draw a picture that represents their insight or action.

There are many ways to use annotation tools during a virtual class. One of my favorites is to create a grid on screen, and allow participants to choose a grid space to personalize in response to a question. Once participants have selected their spot (by typing their name or some other identifying mark), then I'll ask them to respond to a question.

Figure 3-4 Adobe Connect Draw Tools

Whiteboard

A virtual whiteboard is similar to classroom chart paper or whiteboard. It's a blank screen that can be typed, written, or drawn upon using the program's annotation tools. Whiteboards are typically used for brainstorming and other class drawing activities that engage participants.

Although the whiteboard screen starts as a blank page, a facilitator can set it up ahead of time by adding drawings or other marks for an activity. For instance, they might draw two straight lines to divide the whiteboard into three sections and place a question or word to distinguish each one. They would then ask participants to fill in details.

In one of my class activities, I ask participants to think about benefits to three groups: employees, managers, and the organization. I use a divided whiteboard with one of the three group names at the top of each column. Participants then type on screen to brainstorm the benefits.

As you review the whiteboard capabilities of your virtual training platform, check to see which participant annotation privileges can be granted. Also check to see if there are any limitations to how many participants can annotate at one time and how many whiteboards can be open or shared during a session.

Figure 3-5 Adobe Connect Whiteboard With Annotations

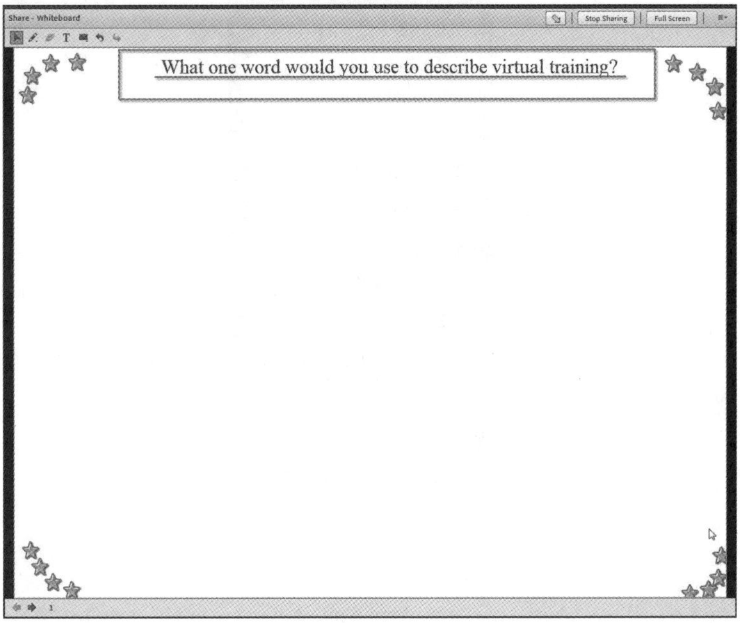

Status Indicators/Raise Hand

Participants who use this feature are able to click on a button to raise their hand or indicate a particular status such as "agree," "disagree," "laughter," or "stepped away." This feature is often used for responding to closed-ended questions and quick yes/no polls. In some platforms, only the facilitator can see the status change or vote of the participants. Other platforms allow everyone to see the hand raised or status change.

Facilitators often use this feature to get a quick response from every participant. For example, when showing a software demonstration, they might ask, "Who has used this feature before? If you have, please 'raise your hand.'" Or the facilitator might ask, "Who agrees with this statement? Click the agree button if you do."

A facilitator can also quickly read the group using this feature. If participants are working on a short individual activity, then the facilitator might say, "Click on the agree button as soon as you finish the exercise, that way I will know you are ready to move on." Once the majority of participants have responded, the facilitator can continue to the next activity.

Figure 3-6 Adobe Connect Status Indicator

Polling

Polls are used to ask real-time survey questions of participants. The questions can be multiple-choice, multiple answer, or in some programs, open-ended text responses. Polls can be used to question participants' in an unlimited number of ways. They can:

- quiz participants' knowledge and understanding of a topic

- generate discussion using opinion questions

- solicit feedback from participants.

Some virtual classroom software programs allow for multiple questions in the same poll. Other programs limit each poll to one question only, but allow you to have more than one poll open at a time. In addition, some platforms allow you to create polls prior to the session and store them as separate files that can be uploaded to the classroom when needed.

Polling questions can be a fun way to engage participants during class. For example, you might create a contest with points awarded for every correct answer, and the person or team with the most points at the end wins a "virtual prize." Or, you can pose a case study scenario related to the content and ask participants via poll to select the character's correct course of action.

Figure 3-7 Adobe Connect Poll

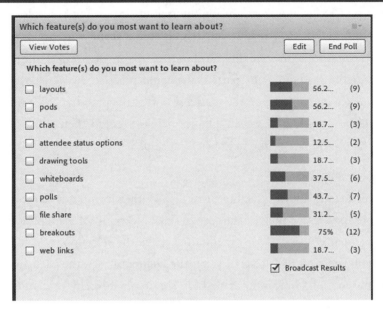

Breakouts

Breakout groups mimic small group activities in the face-to-face classroom. They allow participants to divide into smaller groups to complete a learning exercise such as a skills practice or brainstorm activity. For example, a class with 15 participants might split into three teams of five people each.

The number of breakout rooms available depends upon the virtual classroom software. Some platforms allow only five breakouts while others allow up to 25 or more. Note that if you are using an audio conference in conjunction with your training platform, you will have access to the lowest number of breakouts available from the combination. In other words, if your software allows for 25 breakout rooms but the integrated audio conference only allows 15 audio sub-conferences, then only 15 breakout rooms would be fully available during the session.

During breakouts, participants move into a virtual private meeting room where they only hear their own private conversations with each other. They can share documents and whiteboards among themselves and collaborate together. The facilitator has the ability to move in and out of the breakouts, just like they would walk around the room to check on small groups in an in-person session.

Breakout groups help enable engagement and small group discussion. They can be used to practice skills learned during the training event. For example, if the class learns techniques for how to start a coaching conversation with an employee, the individuals could then practice those techniques in a small group setting.

In a practice breakout, one participant could practice the new coaching skill, another participant could be on the receiving end of the practice, and a third participant could be the silent observer. The participants could then rotate roles, each having a chance to practice the new coaching skill.

Application Sharing

Application sharing allows a facilitator to display their computer screen to participants. More specifically, they can choose to share a certain software program, a web browser, or their entire desktop. Facilitators make the selection, and then participants visually see it on their screen. What the facilitator sees, the participants see.

The purpose of application or desktop sharing is typically to demonstrate the features of a software program or to share a website. For example, participants could learn how to enter numbers into a new expense report form by watching it demonstrated on screen.

Another use of application or desktop sharing could be to display a file that is not compatible with the document sharing feature of the virtual classroom platform. Many presenters will use this as a workaround to the platform when needed.

Other Software

Your organizations may need to consider additional software for use in an online blended curriculum. One of these programs could be a learning management system (LMS) or other database that tracks organizational learning. A LMS can automate many of the administrative processes that surround virtual training (which we'll cover in chapter 7).

Another program that might be used in a blended curriculum is an internal discussion board or social media platform. This system could help create community among participants of a blended curriculum, giving them a place and space to communicate with each other between programs.

Which Comes First?

Which comes first—choosing software or choosing features? It's like asking which comes first, the chicken or the egg? The answer to that question is "yes." The choice can happen either way. They both have their pros and their cons. It's my preference to determine which features are desired first and then choose software accordingly.

Internet Bandwidth

The hardware, audio, and software come together over the Internet to create a virtual training class. And so therefore, the Internet connectivity should also be factored into the technology equation. Without a stable, reliable connection with suitable bandwidth for your needs, your virtual training will not be successful.

The Internet bandwidth availability for each participant should be broad enough to support the class activities. There is nothing worse than a participant who continuously gets disconnected from a class because their Internet connection is not strong enough. The participant gets frustrated and wastes time re-logging in. The facilitator or producer may have to stop and work with that person to get them reconnected. Other participants may be negatively affected while they wait for class to get back on track. Maybe a worse scenario is when a participant stays connected to the class, but due to limited bandwidth they have trouble seeing the screen or watching a video playback. That experience, from the participant point of view, is extremely frustrating. It's like knowing that everyone else is eating a tasty meal while they only get leftover crumbs.

Some software platforms have built-in bandwidth buffers, and play the audio at the same download rate as the participant bandwidth. Other platforms allow the host to change meeting room connectivity speeds to match the anticipated Internet bandwidth.

Bandwidth typically becomes an issue when participants log in from a spotty, publically shared Wi-Fi connection. The best remedy for this issue is to instruct participants ahead of time on best practices for connecting to a virtual class (see chapter 6 for more details). However, Internet bandwidth may also be an issue at a corporate location when the following factors may be true:

- multiple participants connect at the same time from the same location

- a virtual class makes heavy use of multimedia, such as sharing video

- other business functions tie up bandwidth during certain timeframes.

To mitigate any Internet bandwidth issues that may occur and disrupt virtual training, you should thoroughly test Internet connectivity issues by replicating the exact conditions under which it will be needed. At the same time of day, with a similar number of users, and so on. You should also make use of any features found in the virtual software platform that help control bandwidth.

Figure 3-8 Adobe Connect Meeting Preferences—Bandwidth

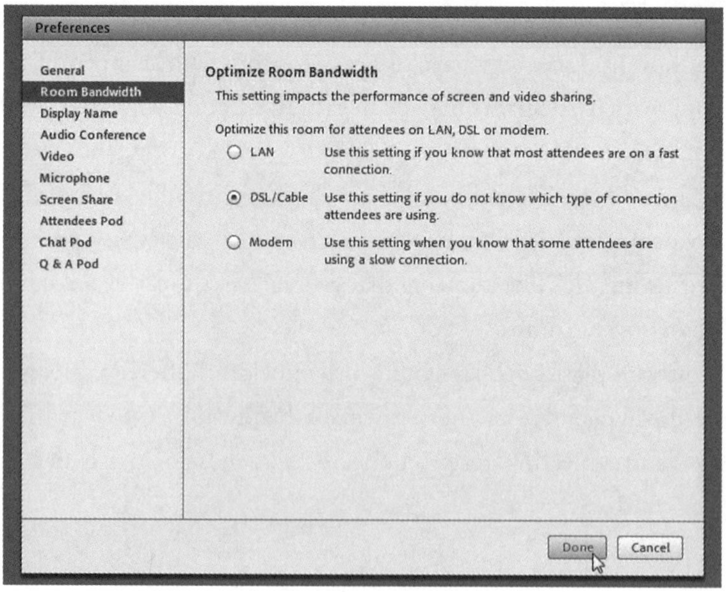

Partnering With IT to Select Technology

"IT Is From Venus, Non-IT Is From Mars" was a headline article in an April 2012 article in the *Wall Street Journal.* The author, George Westerman, a research scientist at MIT, has studied communication between information technology (IT) and other parts of organizations. He recommends, among other things, increased communication and transparency, which will lead to better success for all.

This truth can be applied to the relationship between training professionals and IT, especially when rolling out virtual training. The more communication and transparency you have with the IT department, the more successful your virtual training implementation will be.

In most organizations, IT has control over which software programs everyone has access to. Even in a bring-your-own-device work environment, where employees can use personal technology for work related tasks, the IT department grants access to company systems and software programs. Therefore, you must establish a good relationship with IT decision makers and discuss your training requirements with them. If the IT department purchases a web-based platform, you want it to be one that fits the organization's training needs.

Virtual trainers frequently say, "Our IT department made the decision for us. We will be using such-and-such software." And so often I hear online trainers say, "Our IT department purchased the 'meeting' version of the virtual software and I'm trying to convince them to upgrade to the 'training' version of it." Nip this problem in the bud by working together with the IT team to make a purchasing decision that's right for everyone.

"Partnering with IT can make or break you. You need their support and buy in to be successful with virtual training."

—Wendy Gates Corbett, Global Training Director

So the question probably on your mind is, "How do I partner with IT?" Which is a similar question to, "How do I create a working relationship with someone?" The best way to build a relationship is to start communicating, start listening, and build trust. Find a person in the IT group who is willing to partner with you. Begin by inviting discussion around common goals and needs. When training professionals look for software solutions, they often look to features and benefits first. They'll ask, "What can the software do to help our participants learn?" "Does it have such-and-such feature that we want to have?"

On the flip side, IT will have a different perspective on considering software solutions. They will ask questions such as:

- Will it work with our already existing systems? Is it compatible?

- Will we buy and install it, or will it be hosted by a vendor?

- If we buy it, who will install it? Maintain it? Support it?

- If it's hosted, will the hosting company protect our data?

- What IT resources—initially and ongoing—will be needed?

When you partner together with IT to make your technology selections—hardware, and software—you will end up with a choice that appeals to both sides. You will also have a working partnership that will strengthen your virtual training implementation.

"When deciding upon a software solution for training, check to see what already exists in the organization. You may discover a solution in use by another area that would fit your need without needing to make an additional purchase. Or if an existing solution does not quite fit because it's lacking a feature or doesn't do what you want, then work together with IT and the rest of the organization to find a solution that is a better fit for all parties."

—Tracy Stanfield, a seasoned IT professional

One Organization's Story

Ken Hubbell, Senior Manager of Learning Technology at Ingersoll Rand, said, "When we first started, our learning group did not talk to IT. And IT only came to us when we pushed bandwidth limits. We had very little communication, and then only if there were problems." Ken realized that it would be better to create a conversational network between the departments—IT, Communication, and Learning. He saw that they all used the same tools, and thought it would make sense to communicate about them. "It's important for us to 'sing off of the same song sheet' and not place demands on the system at the same time."

So he invited representatives from each group to meet together monthly. This opened the conversation around needs, desires, and shared goals. It also led to the creation of a technology forecast, which helped ensure that learning wasn't getting too far ahead of IT. The group looks at where they are today, where they will be in a year, and where they will be in the future. Their goal is to be ready, to be informed, and to be aligned.

Selecting a Technology Vendor

If you're selecting a virtual classroom platform "from scratch"—meaning your organization doesn't currently have a provider and you're in the market for a new platform, then do what you would do when purchasing a new vehicle: do your research, shop around, ask for recommendations, read the user reviews, take a few test drives, and sit in both the driver and the passenger seat. In other words, do your homework and take your time in making a decision. Experience the platform from both the facilitator and the participant views. Ask current users for their recommendations and advice. Figuring out which virtual platform to use is kind of like figuring out which car to buy...they all have similar features and everyone has their personal preference.

You can do your own research and comparison several ways. First, by participating in sessions offered by each vendor. Most offer free sessions to help you learn the features of their program. Second, by signing up for trial versions of the platforms. Most offer 30-day trials. Third, by searching on the web for comparative information. I'm often asked, "What's the best platform on the market today"? Or, "Which platform should we choose?" My answer is always the same: "It depends." It's also like purchasing a vehicle. They all have the same basic purpose, with have varying styles and options. Everyone has their own favorite brand.

My best advice is to start with a list of features you need in a virtual platform. Do you need breakout groups so that you can have small group activities? Do you need video streaming for demonstrations? Do you need a private chat option for the type of communication you plan to use? Do you need compatibility with a specific LMS? All of these features will help you narrow down which vendor's virtual training platform will be the best fit for your organization.

Another consideration will be whether you will partner directly with the platform provider, or if you will go through a third-party reseller. Resellers typically offer additional services to support the programs, such as training, technical support, and event management. They may also package together audio conferencing and web conferencing into one bundled solution.

The decision to use a third party vendor versus going straight to a platform vendor will depend upon your organization's overall web conferencing needs. On the one hand, if you need both audio and web conferencing, the third party vendors often provide integrated solutions. On the other hand, you may not need all of the services offered through these bundles. It's important for you to research thoroughly and decide appropriately.

When partnering with any vendor, either a software company or a reseller, use the following common-sense guidelines:

- Create a request for proposal (RFP), either formal or informal, to document what you need and want out of a vendor solution.

- Invite a company representative to demonstrate their software.

- Request a trial version of the program.

- Ask for client references, and contact them for details.

Once you have selected a virtual training platform, you will be able to design, deliver, and implement virtual training classes.

One Organization's Story

When Stephan Girard, Director of Workforce Development at PMMI was searching for a virtual training platform, he had two big selection criteria. First, the cost had to fit within budget. The investment needed to be the right amount based on their planned usage of the platform. Second, since the participants would come from many organizations and could have various computer configurations, Stephan had to assume that they might not have administrative rights to install software. Therefore, the criterion was no software downloads or plug-ins needed for participants. It would be fine for the facilitators to install software, but not the participants.

By honing in on these two important items, Stephan was able to narrow down his choices and work with a vendor to select the right solution for PMMI.

In Summary: Key Points From Chapter 3

- Partner with your organization's IT department to select technology.

- Each person connecting to a virtual training session needs to have their own computer connection. At the time of this writing, mobile devices have limited virtual classroom functionality.

- One of your most important decisions will be to choose which vendor's product you will use for virtual training. Will it be a "meeting" product or a "training" product? Select the one that's most closely aligned to your definition of virtual training.

- Most platforms have similar features and tools. Find out which ones are available in your platform.

- Test Internet bandwidth for all facilitators and participants to ensure connectivity.

Checklist 3-1 Technology

Participant

Hardware:

 ○ Computer or laptop

Audio:

 ○ Hands-free headset

 ○ Reliable telephone connection or VoIP

Software:

 ○ Required downloads or plug-ins for virtual platform

Internet connection:

 ○ Speed test for appropriate bandwidth

Facilitator/Producer

Hardware:

 ○ Computer or laptop

 ○ Second computer or laptop

Audio:

 ○ Hands-free headset

 ○ Reliable telephone connection or VoIP

Software:

 ○ Required downloads or plug-ins for virtual platform

Internet connection:

 ○ Speed test for appropriate bandwidth

** Note that the facilitator may also need to plan for redundancies in telephony and possibly Internet connection, in case of unexpected technical issues. For example, if the facilitator works from a home office, they should have a backup telephone (such as a mobile device) and an alternate internet connection (such as an air card or nearby Wi-Fi hotspot).

Checklist 3-2 Criteria Grid to Help Select a Virtual Training Platform

Features	Vendor 1	Vendor 2	Vendor 3	Vendor 4
Platform Features				
Shared documents: file types	O	O	O	O
Media file playback (audio and/or video)	O	O	O	O
Chat	O	O	O	O
Annotation/drawing privileges	O	O	O	O
Whiteboard features	O	O	O	O
Raise hand/status indicators	O	O	O	O
Breakout groups	O	O	O	O
Other:	O	O	O	O
Audio Features				
Integrated conference calling available?	O	O	O	O
VoIP available?	O	O	O	O
Other Features				
Compatible with mobile devices (for participants)?	O	O	O	O
Able to have multiple hosts/facilitators?	O	O	O	O
Compatible with your organization's LMS?	O	O	O	O
Internet bandwidth requirements:	O	O	O	O
Other Considerations Unique to Your Organization				
	O	O	O	O
	O	O	O	O
	O	O	O	O
	O	O	O	O
	O	O	O	O
	O	O	O	O

Chapter (4)

Design Content

In this chapter, you will learn how to design virtual training:

- Learn three virtual design basics.
- Review a three-step virtual training design model.
- Create virtual course materials.

Virtual training has gotten a poor reputation because many people think it's boring and not an engaging way to learn. They may have attended a lecture-style webcast, or they can't imagine how they could meaningfully interact with others online.

Your success with virtual training will depend upon well-designed classes. A design that engages participants, creates a comfortable space for learning, and helps them apply a new skill. Good design is more than just posting slides online and clicking through them while someone talks. It's about creating a high-quality learning experience.

This chapter will give an overview of best practice virtual training design principles, teach you a three-step design process, and give tips for converting traditional courses to the online classroom. It will also cover techniques for creating virtual course materials.

Basics of Virtual Training Design

The first decision to make related to design is what type of session you will offer. By making this very deliberate choice with intention, you set the design foundation of a meaningful quality learning experience for participants.

In chapter 2, you learned the different definitions of virtual training. Naturally, your design will flow from your definition of virtual training. Think about it—the design of a 15-person virtual training class will be different than the design for a 75-person webinar. And the design of a small virtual meeting will be different than the design of a webcast with 2,000 people.

*"When someone comes to our design team with a training request, we conduct
a needs assessment to determine our design approach. Based on the topic, the
logistics, and the audience, we design different types of virtual experiences. We set
expectations of what the learners will receive, from a webinar that has very little
participation to an extremely interactive blended solution that includes engaging
virtual classes. We distinguish between webinars and virtual training based on the
level of interactivity and how immersed the participant will be in the learning."*

—Peggy Page, Design Group Manager, TD Bank

Here are three basic design considerations for a virtual training session:

- class size

- frequency of interaction

- timing.

Class Size

Most training classes are kept small to allow for meaningful discussion and facilitator observation and feedback of skill practice. I've asked hundreds of trainers to tell me their typical in-person training class sizes, and the most common range is between 10 and 25 participants.

One advantage of moving to the online environment is the ability to reach a larger audience. Virtual platforms allow for hundreds and even thousands of participants to connect at one time. But just because you can put hundreds of people into a virtual training class, doesn't mean you should.

In John Medina's well-researched book *Brain Rules*, he advocates for smaller class sizes because they have better learning environments. A teacher can pay more attention to each individual student, which likely contributes to better student performance (Medina, 2008, 67). We can apply this same education principle to the virtual classroom—the smaller the class size, the better the learning outcome.

There are most certainly times when large numbers of participants in an online session is a good thing. If your goal is to present information in a webcast format, with one or two people presenting and doing all of the talking, then go for a large number of participants. You can achieve economies of scale when holding this type of online meeting. For example, if your sales organization wants to reach the masses to announce a new product on the market, then it makes sense to broadcast this information to the largest audience possible. Or, if your organization needs to quickly hold a town-hall meeting with its worldwide workforce, then a large-scale event would be appropriate. Or, if you bring in a panel of subject matter experts to share their latest findings on a topic of interest to a large audience, then make use of virtual event technology to make it happen. Remember, however, our definition of virtual training. You must distinguish between these large webcast events and virtual training classes. There is a difference.

If a training class is designed for 20 people, then the training class is designed for 20 people whether it's in a face-to-face or online format. If you increase the participant numbers then you are likely to lose the interactivity, the discussion opportunities, and the ability to easily coach participants on the new skills. Don't upsize your training just because you can. Upsize only when it makes sense to do so—if the topic permits and your design allows for it. For virtual training, my recommendation is to keep your class numbers to a manageable level, ideally under 15 participants per session.

Frequency of Interaction

Virtual training must engage participants through frequent, meaningful activities that keep their attention. And it's not only about frequent interaction—responding to one poll question after another will get boring fast. It's also important to be mindful about the variety of interaction and the creative use of virtual tools in the course design.

Based on what we know about adult learners, and our own experience, there is only so much lecture that can be absorbed at one time. And lecture is one of the least effective ways to learn a new skill. (When was the last time you paid full attention to a lengthy lecture? And even if you responded "recently," did that single lecture increase your skill or make you an expert in that topic?) Most adults learn best through hands-on interaction and practice over time.

A recent study by physics Nobelist Carl Wieman and a team at the University of British Columbia compared results between learners who listened to lectures and those who participated in an interactive lesson. The differences were dramatic, and the study confirmed that "learning only happens when you have...intense engagement" (cited in Mervis, 2011).

On top of these truths about adult learning, now add the virtual classroom. Participants who already have short attention spans are now being asked to stay at their desks, use their own computers, and connect to a virtual classroom. The short attention span combined with the distractions all around can be a recipe for virtual training disaster.

But it can be done. With a well-designed virtual training class, participants can stay fully engaged and learn something new. My favorite compliment to receive from a participant after a virtual training class is, "I was so engaged, I didn't have time to check my email during class." This enthusiastic response is largely achieved through a design with frequent, meaningful interactions.

We'll talk much more about helping participants manage their own distractions in chapter 6. For now, let's stay focused on what we should do in the class design to create an interactive learning environment.

Most experienced virtual class designers will tell you that participants in virtual classes should interact at least every three to five minutes. This interaction can be with the virtual tools, with another participant, or with the facilitator. It means that the participants are actively doing something—beyond listening to someone else speak—every few minutes.

Training leader Bob Pike, in his seminal work, *Creative Training Techniques Handbook*, states that in the in-person classroom, "…participants can listen with understanding for 90 minutes, listen with retention for 20 minutes, and that we need to involve them every eight minutes" (2002, 218). When applying this same principle to the virtual classroom, he cuts this time in half and advises involving participants at least every four minutes (2011).

This number is rooted in brain-based research as well as practical experience. Another of John Medina's brain rules is that "people don't pay attention to boring things" (2008, 94). Participants will check out at least every 10 minutes unless you give them compelling reasons to stay tuned into the class. Connect the fact that learners have a hard time paying attention to the multitude of extra distractions that participants have in their own environment where you can't see them, and you will discover that frequent, meaningful virtual class activities are a must.

The bottom line is that you need to design virtual classes for maximum learning interaction, at least every few minutes.

Timing

According to research conducted by The eLearning Guild among its members, 92 percent of their virtual training classes are between 30 to 120 minutes in length. This breaks down further into 51 percent of classes are between 30-60 minutes, and 41 percent of classes are between 60 to 120 minutes (Shank, 2010). One main reason for this short length of time is to help avoid cognitive overload. By chunking a training event down into manageable pieces, participants will be better able to learn and retain content.

I'm often asked about the overall length of a virtual training program—if it could be five, six, or even eight hours in length. Imagine this timing from a participant perspective—sitting at a desk, glued to the computer, interacting every three to four minutes, for hours upon end. Most people couldn't sustain that attention span, even with the most interesting content. To keep participants fresh, comfortable, and open to learning, virtual sessions should be in short bursts of highly interactive time; 45 to 60 minutes is ideal, 90 to 120 minutes is maximum.

Even these longer 90 to 120 sessions should include a break. If you don't take a physical and mental break at least every 60 minutes, the participants will take one anyway. They will check out when they need to. And depending on when that is, they could possibly miss the most important learning point of the session. Avoid this by designing sessions with an eye on the clock and your participants' attention spans.

For example, in the middle of my classes I often ask participants to stand up and stretch, then sit back down and "raise their hand" in the platform to indicate they are ready to continue. This brief physical and mental break only takes a few seconds yet refreshes everyone. And in a longer session, I might set an on-screen timer for five minutes, ask participants to stay connected to the session, but allow for a formal opportunity for everyone to step away from their computer. When the timer ends, so does the break.

Since virtual training classes are often part of a blended learning program, an overall curriculum might contain several short sessions strung together over time. So the overall time for a class may be many hours, but they are spread out with plentiful breaks in between. In other words, class might meet for two hours each afternoon on Tuesday, Wednesday, and Thursday. Or the class might meet for six consecutive Fridays at 10 a.m. for 90 minutes each time.

If you are converting an in-person training class to the virtual classroom, know that your timing will most likely be shortened in comparison. Virtual classes usually move at a faster pace due to the use of platform tools. Moving at a faster pace also helps keep participants engaged in the learning content. In addition, your activity timeframes will shorten for most in-person exercises that are converted to the virtual classroom. For example, a traditional face-to-face class might call for participants to watch a software demonstration, answer questions about what they saw, and then try it on their own. This classroom sequence might take 45 minutes. Yet in the virtual classroom, if those same questions are asked via polling, and multiple polls are displayed on screen at the same time, this section would move at a faster pace. The overall activity might only take 20 to 30 minutes in the virtual classroom.

In another example, in a face-to-face class, you might have participants "go around the room" and introduce themselves one-by-one. But in the virtual classroom, participants can type their introductions simultaneously in the chat window. The face-to-face introductions could take upwards of 20 minutes, while the online chat introductions might only take two minutes.

These three basic design considerations—size, interaction, and timing—should be factored into all of your virtual training design decisions.

Converting Lengthy Classes to the Virtual Classroom

A common question I frequently hear is "How do you convert a lengthy face-to-face class into a virtual one?" For example, what should you do if you start with a two-week orientation program? Or a six-week in-depth technical series? In these cases, you would still follow the same process: select the best format for each learning objective, shape appropriate learning activities, and structure a logical flow. You will most likely break apart the training class into many smaller chunks. The two-week orientation may become 10 live online sessions with assignments in-between. The six-week technical series may become a shorter face-to-face class, with follow-on virtual sessions and on-the-job coaching. Again, your possibilities are endless provided that you engage participants in their own learning using all available tools.

A Virtual Training Design Model

Based upon my experience designing many interactive virtual training classes, this is the three-step design process that I follow and have found to be successful:

1. Select the best format for each learning objective.

2. Shape appropriate learning activities.

3. Structure a logical flow.

Step 1: Select the Best Format for Each Learning Objective

For any training design to be successful, you start with the learning objectives. What do learners need to know or do at the end of the session? What skills should they have? What changed behavior should there be? What do they need to start doing? Or stop doing?

By focusing on the learning objectives, you have a sense of what needs to be covered in the virtual training curriculum. One way or another, the learning objectives reveal your end goal and what you want your learners to accomplish. By starting with the learning objectives, you will establish a solid foundation of what belongs in the virtual training class. You will also be able to differentiate between "need to know" and "nice to know" information.

"Every time I design a virtual class, I ask, 'What do the participants need to know to do their job?' Then, when looking at content and materials, I ask, 'Is it necessary for participants to do this in class? Where's the value?' If there is no value in doing it in a group setting, then there's no value in including it in the virtual class."

—Jennifer Newton, Instructional Designer

Once the learning objectives are confirmed, you then select the best format for each one. By *format*, I mean it in the broadest sense of the word: the basic design plan for the class. Or, in other words, the delivery modality for the content. When considering the format, I ask questions such as: What's the best way for a participant to learn that content? Could they simply read a document and have enough understanding of the topic to act upon it? Or does the content warrant a discussion with a subject matter expert or practice in a simulated environment?

This is one of the greatest benefits of virtual training—its flexibility. The ability to mix and match various learning formats into one training curriculum. You can combine asynchronous assignments with synchronous events to make a full program. There is no rule that says "you must put everything into one long continuous virtual training class." It's actually the opposite. You might have four virtual sessions that make up a series, or two virtual sessions with a learning assignment in-between, or any other combination of components. You can break down larger pieces into smaller chunks of learning and then arrange them in the best way possible.

For example, last year I designed a change management curriculum that included two virtual classes, one in-person class, and two on-the-job application assignments. The overall program was spread out over 12 weeks to give participants time to apply what they were learning in-between each session.

When this type of design is done well, it's an art form. It's like a child's building block set that can be pulled apart and put together in many different ways. When you build a curriculum, you put the learning chunks together in ways that make the most sense to your learners and the content at hand.

There are four main questions to ask when choosing the "best" or the most appropriate format for each learning objective:

- What is the type of learning objective?

- Is togetherness required?

- What are the technology capabilities?

- What are the trainees' backgrounds?

Let's review each of these "4 Ts" (type, togetherness, technology, trainees) in more detail.

What Is the Type of Learning Objective?

As I mentioned above, the learning objectives will tell you which topics belong in the virtual session, and which topics can be moved to another type of assignment or out of the curriculum altogether.

If the learning objective only requires recognition or rudimentary comprehension, then that topic may not need to be covered during the live online class. It might fit better into a pre-session reading assignment, or a post-session activity. For example, if participants need to identify parts of a machine before they can operate it, then they could learn this fundamental knowledge by watching a video prior to class or navigating through a self-paced lesson. Or if participants need to recognize which type of eye protection to wear when performing a specific maintenance task, then they could learn to identify it by reading a job aid.

While it may sound complicated, you are probably very familiar with this model of taking knowledge objectives out of the classroom. For example, you may have had this experience when you learned how to drive a vehicle. You first needed to have a general understanding of traffic signs and learn basic rules of the road, and then needed to learn the actual skill of driving. Most of us learned the general knowledge through reading the booklet available through our state's transportation office, and then learned the skill of driving through hands-on practice.

Or, maybe you experienced this model instead when learning how to cook. You started with the basics—reading a recipe on a package, identifying and selecting the necessary kitchen tools, and learning the fundamental mixing and stirring techniques. Many of these basics were learned on your own by reading a cookbook, by observing someone else in the kitchen, or by watching videos of your favorite television chef. At some point, you applied this knowledge to a hands-on kitchen experience, either under the guidance of an experienced teacher or through trial and error. The fundamental knowledge was acquired on your own, and then applied in a hands-on setting.

To apply this principle to your virtual training design, look at the objectives to see what a participant simply needs to know or understand. Do they have to identify parts of a spreadsheet in order to enter data into it? Or select the correct form to use when a customer files a complaint? Or to recognize which questions can and cannot be asked during a hiring interview? For these, and other knowledge-only learning objectives, consider turning them into a self-paced activity that the participant is required to do on their own time. Of course, there are times when it makes sense to keep a knowledge objective in a class. For example, when the topic is short and you can quickly review it during class time, or it's complicated enough that participants need to be able to ask questions while learning it.

When considering the type of learning objectives you have for your curriculum, remember that a virtual training class is very often part of a blended design, with the knowledge only objectives as asynchronous self-paced assignments and the skill and application objectives addressed in the synchronous virtual classroom.

Effective Learning Objectives

The best learning objectives are ones that specifically tie to what learners need to know or do on the job. According to Julie Dirksen's fantastic book, *Design for How People Learn*, well-written learning objectives should indicate "something the learner would actually do in the real world" and something you can "tell when they've done it" (2012, 65).

Even if you have a situation where knowledge is the outcome, there is usually some way that learners need to act upon that knowledge. Therefore, actions in your learning objectives should be an active verb. One sign of a weak learning objective is the use of "know" or "understand" as the verb, because neither of those actions can be measured.

To illustrate, consider the difference between these examples:

"At the end of this training session, a participant will know three techniques for responding to an upset customer."

Or

"At the end of this training session, a participant will be able to:

- recognize three techniques for responding to upset customers
- select an appropriate technique based upon an upset customer's situation
- use the appropriate technique to respond to an upset customer."

Notice how the second example is much richer, ties to what the learner would need to do on the job, and enables you to plan out in more detail what the training program needs to cover.

Is Togetherness Required?

The next consideration is to ask: Would participants benefit from being together to learn this particular objective? If so, then the topic may be best addressed during the live online session.

It could be that your topic naturally assumes participants will be together. Interpersonal skills such as communication or negotiation skills need to be practiced in tandem with someone else. Or you might have a topic where it would benefit learners to have synchronous live discussion with a facilitator or each other. Maybe the topic is complicated and requires significant amounts of explanation. Or maybe the topic is sensitive and could result in emotional reactions from participants that are best talked through.

For example, there might be a brand new standard operating procedure that requires participants to learn the procedure, and also to have a willingness to change from the old procedure. You know that there could be resistance to this change, and want to have the participants be able to talk through it and mentally process the new procedure together with others. When participants will benefit from being together, it makes sense to have this learning objective in the synchronous virtual session design.

What Are the Technology Capabilities?

Next, consider the technology capabilities within your organization and of your participants. Some of your virtual training design will be driven by these technology opportunities and limitations.

In the last chapter, we addressed selecting a technology platform based upon your organization's needs. So hopefully the virtual training platform will not be a limitation. However, the reality is that sometimes the technology factors into the choices you make about the virtual training class design. For example, if you wish to have participants watch a demonstration video clip but their computers don't have sound cards to hear the audio, then you might need to determine another way, such as show still screen shots, to show the demonstration and have the facilitator verbally talk through it. Or let's say you wish for participants to practice a new skill by role playing in small groups. If your selected virtual classroom platform does not support breakout groups, then you might design the training as a blended curriculum: assign small groups to meet on their own after a virtual class, and then report back to the large group during the next session.

As we discussed in the last chapter, to ensure that your technology capabilities match your training needs, partner closely together with your organization's IT department to select and implement the appropriate technology.

What Are the Trainees' Backgrounds?

The final important consideration in the design format is to think about the typical participants who will be in the virtual classes, and design with them in mind. For example, do participants have limited time available during the day to attend training? That restriction may influence the length of your sessions. You may realize it's better to hold three 90-minute sessions on the same day, with plenty of break time in-between. Or you may determine that it would be better for your participants to have five 45-minute sessions spread out over several weeks.

Are your participants going to be brand new to virtual training? Then plan your format to build in a basic activity to help them learn how to use a tool before asking them to use it for a complex learning topic. For example, help participants get comfortable typing to everyone in the chat window during introductions, and then introduce the more complicated private chat feature for a paired discussion activity later in the session. Or, do your participants speak another language? If so, then you might need to allow for extra reading and typing time during a session. Or you might need to include a glossary of terms along with the participant materials, allowing global participants time to look up unfamiliar words prior to class.

Once you consider these factors, you can select the appropriate format for each learning objective. This process will form the foundation and structure of your virtual training program.

Converting Learning Objectives

If you are converting an in-person class to a virtual one, and you discover it doesn't have learning objectives, or the learning objectives don't really describe what a participant needs to do back on the job—then go back to the analysis phase of the ADDIE model to determine what your learners need to know or do.

In fact, it's a good idea to go back and revisit the learning objectives of your traditional training class anyway before you convert it to a live online one. Maybe you just quickly review each one with a subject matter expert and check to see that they are still valid. This short review may uncover more significant challenges that can be addressed before converting to the live online format.

For example, when Danielle Buscher, Director of Global Learning at Marriott International, worked with her team to convert a traditional classroom curriculum to a blended one, they took the time to partner with subject matter experts to ensure the class messages were engaging, relevant, and up to date. While this step took extra design time, it resulted in an exceptional virtual training program.

Step 2: Shape Appropriate Learning Activities

Once you have used the learning objectives to determine which topics to cover within a virtual training session, the next step is to select appropriate activities that lead to their accomplishment.

The process of selecting activities for virtual training is very similar to designing a traditional in-person class. Design a learning experience that incorporates adult learning methods and real-world application. Motivate participants to learn by helping them see the importance of content. Find participant-centered ways to present content, and provide relevant practice opportunities.

This isn't a book on instructional design basics—so I'll assume you have a foundational knowledge in it that you can apply when selecting learning activities. If instructional design is not your strong point, check out the resource list found at the end of this book.

What's important for our purposes in this chapter—and where we will focus in this section—is what's unique about designing for virtual classes. In short, it's the tools available to you in the virtual classroom platform (such as chat or polling) and how you match learning objectives to them.

Ruth Colvin Clark and Ann Kwinn, authors of *The New Virtual Classroom,* put it this way: "Virtual classroom software tools actually offer instructors more opportunities for frequent learner interactions than do most traditional classroom settings. Frequent and effective use of these response facilities is the single most important technique for successful virtual events" (2007, 107). Therefore when looking at your learning outcomes, you select virtual classroom learning tools and methods that enable participants to achieve them.

For instance, let's say participants need to learn how to resolve conflict in a team setting, and the class learning objectives include how to "facilitate a dialogue" and "respond to emotional reactions." You would shape learning activities around these topics. They could learn by watching a video demonstration, discussing their past experience, and practicing real world scenarios. Or they could learn by listening to a brief lecture, working through a case study, and then receive facilitator feedback on practice situations.

There's not one single way to select activities that lead to learning outcomes. Different designers create different designs according to their style, their preference, and their experience. Remember to design engaging activities that drive toward learning outcomes, not just "busy work" for the sake of interactivity. As we established earlier, interactive virtual classes should engage participants at least every few minutes. Use the platform tools to engage participants, and use your creativity to design unique interactions.

Important Point

It's not just about keeping participants busy, it's about engaging them in their own learning.

If you are converting an in-person class, some activities in a traditional training class easily translate into the live online environment. For example, a classroom paired discussion activity could become an online paired chat activity. Or a classroom competition between teams to answer questions could become an online competition using poll questions. And a live demonstration could become a live demonstration using screen sharing capabilities.

Be resourceful when designing activities for the live online classroom. Your use of the tools is only limited by your imagination and creativity. For example, if you usually toss a foam ball from one participant to another in the face-to-face classroom for a "hot potato" type activity, think about how that could be done in the virtual classroom. You might "toss" the virtual ball to the first person by typing their name in the chat window, and then ask them to select the next person, and so on until everyone has been chosen.

Also think about ways participants can use all of the tools available to them. If you use handouts, have participants "raise their hand" when finished with a worksheet exercise. When asking questions, direct participants to respond via chat. When surveying the group, create challenging poll questions to check for knowledge or to get participants thinking. In a recent online survey compiled by Roger Courville of 1080 Group, attendees rated multi-select polling as the most engaging activity in a virtual session (refer to Roger's website, www.thevirtualpresenter.com, for more information about his research). Single-select polling followed close behind. One implication of this study is that your design will be more engaging if you involve them in the content.

Here are some ideas for using some of the common virtual classroom tools. In this example, the topic is collaborative coaching skills for managers. For illustrative purposes, I have provided an example for each tool from a manager's coaching skills class. In reality, we would use these tools over and over again in various ways throughout the entire class.

Tool	Virtual Classroom Activity Idea for a Coaching Class
Share Document	Open a document that contains a written script of a dialogue between a manager and employee. Ask participants to use their annotation tools to highlight words and phrases that should not be used in a collaborative coaching conversation.
Chat	Post a poorly worded example of a manager's coaching statement on screen, and ask participants to rewrite the statement using coaching techniques they just learned.
Media	Show a short prerecorded video example of a manager demonstrating a coaching skill that participants are learning. Prior to the video, ask participants to be on the lookout for specific examples of the skill use and invite them to take notes on their handout or in chat.
Whiteboard Annotation	Ask participants to type challenging statements on screen that employees might say in response during a collaborative coaching conversation. Then categorize these statements (either by color highlight or some other indicator) for use in discussion and practice activity.
Status Indicators	Make a persuasive statement about coaching, and ask participants to indicate agreement or disagreement with the statement by choosing the appropriate status indicator ("raise hand" or "agree"/"disagree").
Poll	Post a list of challenging coaching situations, and ask participants to select all of the ones they have experienced.
Breakouts	Divide participants into groups of three. Assign a role-play exercise where one person plays the manager, one plays the employee, and the third person observes. Have the observer take notes and lead a coaching conversation, before the group switches roles and gives each person a chance to practice.

Table 4-1 Ideas for Using Common Virtual Classroom Tools

Tips for Designing Presentation-Style Webcasts and Webinars

Back in chapter 2, we distinguished between webcasts, webinars, and virtual training classes by the amount of interactivity in each one and the number of typical participants. If you need to apply the virtual training design principles found in this chapter to a presentation-style webcast or webinar design, keep these additional points in mind:

- Find out as much as you can about the audience ahead of time so that you can tailor the content and make it relevant to them.
- Add as much interactivity as possible by making full use of the available web platform features.
- Insert "Question and Answer" segments throughout the session, instead of waiting until the end. For example, instead of a 45-minute lecture with 15 minutes of questions, intersperse the question opportunities throughout.
- Use a webcam for presenters to add a personal touch.
- Make the screen as visually appealing as possible through creative use of slides and graphics. Also, create enough slides so that the on-screen display will change frequently enough to help maintain visual interest.

Content Type

It doesn't matter what type of training you have to deliver virtually: technical, interpersonal, or something unique to your organization. Just about anything can be taught in the live online environment. It's possible to deliver technical training, software training, interpersonal skills training, communication skills, or even sales training using the virtual classroom.

Here are some special activity selection considerations when designing for technical training and interpersonal skills training.

Technical training: It may seem natural to use technology to deliver technical training. The connection seems obvious, doesn't it? However, the reality is not as simple as it seems. It's easy to conduct software demonstrations online, and straightforward to show a website. Yet an engaging interactive training class requires more than just watching a demonstration. Therefore, when delivering technical training in the virtual classroom, try the following:

- Show the software through screen share, demonstrating its features while asking participants to follow along and take guided notes on a handout that you have provided.

- Give a participant the mouse control and let them drive the software.

- Take screen shots of the software. Ask participants, "Where should I click for the next step?" and have them mark on screen using the annotation tools where they would click to perform a function.

- Use real-world (not hypothetical) examples for participants to work through (for example, use the exact form template they will use on the job instead of just a made up one).

- Use frequent poll questions and chat questions to check for comprehension.

- Use a virtual classroom platform that has a "hands-on lab" feature, which allows multiple participants to use the software at the same time.

Interpersonal skills: Conventional wisdom says that you can't learn soft skills using hard devices. But that conventional wisdom doesn't take into account the collaborative nature of the virtual classroom. Given the tools available in most platforms—notably small group breakout rooms—meaningful dialogue and practice conversations can easily happen. So don't shy away from delivering interpersonal skills topics in the virtual classroom. Therefore, when delivering interpersonal skills training in the virtual classroom, such as listening or speaking skills, try the following:

- Ask for participants' experience with the topic, either via poll questions or through small group discussion.

- Set up case study scenarios that participants can relate to, and ask them to weigh in on how they would approach the situation. Do this in both large and small group settings.

- Use a whiteboard for participants to brainstorm challenging ideas.

- Have participants practice in pairs or trios using breakout rooms.

Step 3: Structure a Logical Flow

Once you've established the learning objectives, and selected the best activity for each one, it's time to put the class together in a logical order. This is called the structure of your design.

There are two levels of structure to a virtual training curriculum. First, the big picture structure that determines how many components make up the course. This structure is the exact number of virtual sessions, any offline or self-paced participant assignments, and how these components fit together. The second type of structure details out the flow of each specific virtual training session. It's how the activities flow from one to the next. It's the sequence of learning content within a session.

A typical virtual training class sequence begins with an overview of the content, assessment and practice opportunities for participants, and application exercises for back on the job. Each activity flows naturally from one to the next, in a logical progression for learning. If you have a lot of content, too much to put into one short virtual session, then you should structure the curriculum into a series of sessions as mentioned earlier in the chapter. If you do this, you would sequence them into a logical progression. The amount of time between the sessions depends upon your topic and your audience. It could be three 60-minute sessions in a day with a 60-minute break in between each one, or nine sessions spread out over many weeks. You would structure the curriculum in the way that makes most sense to your content, your participants, and your organization's needs.

When structuring each individual virtual class, there are two areas that require special attention: opening and sequencing.

Opening

When does a virtual class begin? Many would say it begins at the top of the hour or at the scheduled start time. But the truth is that a virtual class begins the moment a participant logs into the virtual classroom.

Actually, backing up a little, participants will begin to form impressions about the virtual class when they first encounter the description and receive communication about it. The invitation, the welcome, and the instructions will also play a part in how the training is perceived. I'll talk more about setting participants up for success before a virtual session in chapter 6. For our purposes in this chapter, recognize that this pre-class communication is part of the design. The designer should think through and plan for this ancillary material as part of the class structure and flow.

So, the virtual class actually starts when a participant joins online. They should be engaged immediately into some type of activity. If the audience is new to the virtual classroom, it could be something simple such as answering a question via chat to learn how that feature works. It could also be responding to a poll question, writing on the whiteboard, or using the status indicators. I call this time the "start before the start." Its purpose is to set the tone for an interactive, engaging virtual class. Its secondary purpose is to teach the participants the virtual platform, if that's needed. The time is not used for learning new content related to the topic, but instead to establish an engaging learning atmosphere.

For example, here is a peak into of one of my "start before the start" screens:

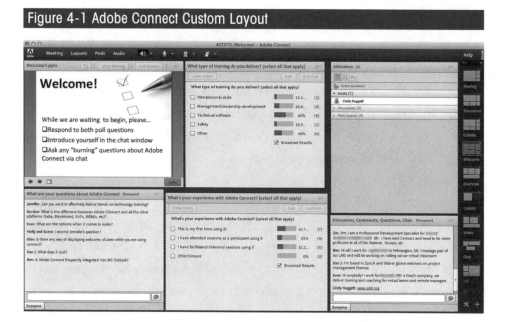

Figure 4-1 Adobe Connect Custom Layout

Then, at the designated class start time, the first learning activity begins. It's important to pay special attention to the opening moments of every virtual session. Within the first few minutes, participants will decide if they will stay engaged or if they will turn their attention to other things. Therefore, plan a meaningful engaging activity within the first few moments of class. Not only will this get your class off on the right foot, it will set the tone for an interactive session.

For example, post an image on screen and ask participants to type out the first three things that come to mind when they see it. Use those words to jump start your conversation about the training topic. Or, at minimum, ask participants to introduce themselves in the chat window and respond to a multi-select poll question that requires some thought before answering.

Sequencing

When sequencing learning events in a class, I follow this simple structure:

- Introduce it.

- Practice it.

- Apply it.

If you are covering multiple topics in a session, this three-part sequence *(introduce it, practice it, apply it)* would repeat over and over again. So if participants are learning how to enter data into an online purchasing system, they would first learn the fundamental process, practice those steps, and then apply them to specific purchasing scenarios they would encounter on the job. This process helps avoid cognitive overload by allowing time to practice and apply before moving to the next topic. It also provides ample opportunity for practice that leads to real-world use back on the job.

While this sequencing pattern is fairly common for designing any type of learning experience, there is a nuance that's unique for virtual classes: the way you incorporate use of virtual platform into the activity flow. For example, when *introducing* a topic, instead of asking overhead-style questions for an open general discussion, it would be better to use directed poll questions for clarity.

Darlene Christopher, Knowledge and Learning Officer at World Bank Group, used this introduction technique in one of her virtual training classes for managers. In order to have a class discussion about what worked in last year's talent management process, she created a poll question that asked participants to anonymously rate on a 1-5 scale how successful they thought last year's process was. This question gave the group a starting point for discussion, which then led into sharing examples of how the process was used. Darlene's design led to much better learning outcomes than she would have gotten by just starting with an open question "So what did everyone think about last year's talent management process?"

For *practice*, make liberal use of the platform's interactive tools for participant feedback opportunities. They can answer questions through the status indicators or a series of poll questions or in a whiteboard activity. Or they could complete worksheet exercises on their own and then compare answers with a partner.

Finally, for *application*, participants would work together in breakout groups on scripted case studies. They could create-their-own practices based upon their prior experience. You could place them into small groups for fishbowl style activities, or have them individually apply new skills and receive feedback from the facilitator. These are just a few brief examples of how to use the tools to engage participants in the learning.

Once you have sketched out the flow of the class, it's important to then look at it through the eyes of your participants. Is there enough variety between platform tools? Does it feel abrupt, or have gradual transitions from one activity to another? You don't want to have six poll questions in a row, or ask them to raise their hand over and over again. It should flow well in terms of activity, variety, as well as logic.

The bottom line is that your sequence, although it shares commonalities with any type of training class, should foster an extremely engaging learning experience for participants. The success of your virtual training class will depend upon it.

Three Conversion Mistakes

There are three common mistakes made when converting traditional in-person training classes to the synchronous live online environment:

1. **Taking an interactive instructor-led classroom session and turning it into a presentation style webcast**. Just because participants are dispersed instead of together doesn't mean that your live online class should be a lecture. Don't forget what you know about adult learning principles and how to engage participants in learning. Those guidelines apply to all types of training, including virtual.

2. **Thinking that an eight-hour instructor led class will be an eight-hour live online virtual session**. The reality is that one minute of classroom time does not equal one minute of virtual time. By using technology you are often able to save time over traditional instructor-led methods. It's one of the many benefits of virtual training.

3. **Inflating the number of participants in the live online class**. Most traditional in person training classes are designed for small numbers of participants. Yet the temptation to vastly increase participant numbers in the equivalent live online class size seems difficult to resist. As I said in the last chapter, just because you can put hundreds of participants in an online classroom, doesn't mean you should.

Creating Virtual Course Materials

Facilitators, producers, and participants depend upon a good design be able to do their jobs well. An interactive virtual class design will set them up for success. In order to help them, you should:

- Create facilitator guides with explicit instructions on how to lead activities.

- Design slides and other visuals to help illustrate lessons and exercises.

- Provide participant handouts with class content (not just a copy of the slides).

Let's look at a few special considerations for each one.

Facilitator Materials

Virtual training facilitator guides tell the trainer and producer exactly what to do for each class activity. Since an interactive design requires action on their part as well, they need to know what is expected of them. The guide can be fully scripted, with instructions for the facilitator to "say" statements and "do" activities. Or they can be simple bullet point lists with general instructions for managing activities. What's most important is the instructions should include enough information for the virtual class activities to run as planned, for the general amount of time expected. Participants should be able to easily complete each learning activity because the facilitator and producer have enough information to make the exercise run smoothly.

If you are both the designer and the facilitator, you might take shortcuts on creating facilitator guides, by using abbreviations and notes that only you understand. However, if anyone besides you will deliver the training program, then you should create a guide for reference and consistency. Also, remember that it's a best practice to have a producer, and they will need to follow along with the instructions as well. Therefore, include notes for the producer as needed.

I have included a sample page from my virtual training facilitator guide template at the end of this chapter, and it's available for download at www.cindyhuggett.com.

Visual Aids

In many virtual classroom software platforms, the largest part of the screen is set aside for document sharing, namely slides. Therefore, the facilitator materials should include at least one set of slides. Remember that virtual training is not the same thing as someone lecturing, presenting, or reading a set of slides. And just because you create slides does not mean that every piece of training content belongs on the slides. It also doesn't mean that the facilitator will read every word on every slide. Instead, the slides have several very specific purposes. First, the slides help present and visually enhance the training content. Second, they help maintain learner attention with interesting graphics and a frequently changing screen. Third, they provide direction and guidance as the class moves through learning activities.

The virtual training slides should be visually appealing. As mentioned earlier, one of John Medina's brain rules is: "We don't pay attention to boring things" (2008, 93). That's a good guideline to remember when designing slides to accompany the facilitator guide.

For more information about good slide design, see the Resources list.

7 Tactics for Virtual Slide Design

By Becky Pike Pluth, President & CEO, The Bob Pike Group

1. Make bullets graphical.
2. Use light background with dark words. It reduces headaches and strain on learners' eyes.
3. Recognize colors speak to emotions. Select colors carefully.
4. Don't limit the number of slides. Put only one idea per slide.
5. Complex content belongs in a handout, not on a slide.
6. Use images, photography, and vector art.
7. Create slides that engage the participant. For example, have a "gallery walk" with four images that represent the information that you are sharing.

© 2013, The Bob Pike Group. Reprinted with permission.

Participant Resources

Participants will benefit from having reference material related to the training class content. This is true in both the in-person classroom and the virtual one. This material can be printed handouts that are sent to participants ahead of time, or via material sharing within the platform.

The purpose of a handout is to keep your participants from needing to write down every key idea or point made during the training class. Handouts (also called participant guides or workbooks) include the main training content, exercises, activity instructions, and reference material. They allow participants to take appropriate notes, just like they would in an in-person class. The handout often includes a job aid that participants will use back in the workplace. Be sure to provide resources, tips, techniques, content, and information that participants will actually use on the job.

"For our single two-hour virtual classes, we provide a PDF document between eight and 20 pages that participants use to fill in and take notes. For longer sessions that mirror our full-day classes, we ship the same materials that participants would receive if they took the in-person program."

—**Treion Muller, Chief eLearning Architect, FranklinCovey**

Print or Ship?

There are two options for sending materials to participants ahead of time. It's most common to send them electronically via email or other electronic distribution system (such as a LMS). This method places the burden on the participants to print the materials, or have them available "on screen" for reference during class. If your handout includes printed worksheets or other activities that require a pen or pencil, be sure to let participants know that they are expected to have a printed hard copy of the handout available for class.

The advantage of sending material electronically is the reduced cost of centrally printed materials—instead the cost burden shifts to the participants as they individually print each document. However, the disadvantage is the potential for participants to not receive the handout ahead of time, or to not print it.

The second option is to ship preprinted materials to participants ahead of time. This option is common when there is a lengthy printed book, or if there is a document with specially formatted pages where it would be difficult for participants to easily print.

The advantage of shipping materials is that you can be relatively sure the participants will receive them in advance of the virtual training class. The disadvantage is the potential high cost of shipping.

Carefully consider which option will work best for your virtual training curriculum.

The participant handout should not be just a copy of the facilitator's slides. The slides will have activity instructions, copies of poll questions, and other items that simply won't be useful for participants' post-class reference. When asked about this topic, my favorite response is that the best slides make the worst handouts.

The slides are part of your facilitator materials. Just like you don't hand over your facilitator guide to participants in an in-person class, you shouldn't send over your facilitator slides in a virtual class. If your participant handout is done well, that should be all that's needed. It will be far more useful than a deck of reference slides.

Designing Participant Materials for a Blended Curriculum

If your virtual training class is one part of a larger program, it would be helpful for participants if you designed a checklist or road map to help them see the big picture of the curriculum. Give them an overview of what to expect, which components they will complete, and any resource requirements (expectations, deadlines, dates and times of synchronous sessions, and so on).

For example, you might create a calendar that shows participants what to do during each week of the curriculum. Or give them a job aid that lists every component of the curriculum and ask them to make notes as they complete each one. The purpose of this participant piece is to guide them through the program. Make it easy for them to follow along.

The beginning of a sample checklist could look something like this:

Week of February 13:

- Introduce yourself on the class portal.
- Attend virtual kickoff meeting with your direct supervisor.
- Begin first assignment (found on the class portal).

Week of February 20:

- Complete first assignment and post responses to portal.
- Meet with your direct supervisor to discuss learning goals for program.
- Attend first class scheduled on Thursday, February 23 at 11 a.m. (link found here).

One Organization's Story

Dan Gallagher, Vice President of Learning at Comcast and author of *The Self-Aware Leader* (ASTD, 2012), converted a two-day traditional classroom-based Performance Management 101 class to the live online environment. The new program included both virtual classes and other self-study components. The live online sessions were held once per week for six weeks, and each one was in the 90-120 minute range. "We took the nugget approach," Dan said, "and we learned many lessons along the way.

"We had to redesign the classroom exercises for the virtual environment. We kept the core learning model, but added new activities and ways to engage the learners.

"Also, while the delivered solution created efficiency for the learners, it increased the amount of work for the trainer and the project manager. We had to create additional documentation for the curriculum.

"Finally, we had to have influence over the class size to keep it to an appropriate level for the curriculum. It's key to manage class size...while you may be able to increase the numbers from a technical perspective, you can't from a learning perspective."

In Summary: Key Points From Chapter 4

- Well-designed virtual training classes are a key to success.
- Design virtual classes for maximum learning interaction, engaging participants at least every 4 minutes.
- It's not about keeping participants busy, it's about engaging them in their own learning.
- A virtual class begins the moment a participant logs into the session, even if that's before the official start time.
- Plan a meaningful engaging activity within the first few moments of a virtual class. Then keep the momentum going with thoughtful activity sequencing.
- Create facilitator and participant materials that are useful for everyone.

Template 4-1 Virtual Training Class Design Document

Time	Objective(s)	Topic	Activity or Learning Method	Materials/Notes
	Pre-class assignment or prep activity			

Source: Adapted from ASTD *Infoline*, "Simple Effective Online Training," by Cindy Huggett and Wendy Gates Corbett (Issue No. 0801).

Template 4-2 Sample Facilitator Guide Page

Welcome and Introductions   **10 minutes**

WELCOME participants the program.

INTRODUCE yourself to the group. Include the following information:
- Your name
- Your location
- Your major responsibilities and trainer experience
- Your role as facilitator of this program

SHOW slide, "Introductions."

HAVE participants introduce themselves using the chat window, sharing the information requested on the slide.

> *Comment on introductions as appropriate. Encourage participants to chat with each other, to begin building a comfortable learning environment.*

SAY:

It looks like we have an eager group who is ready to learn! We will continue using the Chat window, as well as the status indicators and verbal dialogue throughout today's session.

> *If needed, review how to use the status indicators (raise hand, agree, disagree, etc) and how to send public and private chat messages.*

TRANSITION:

Let's take a moment to preview our time together.

Source: www.cindyhuggett.com

Introductions

- Your name
- Your organization
- Your role
- Your location
- Something you hope to gain during this session

Producer Notes:

Introduce yourself in the chat window

Let participants know you're available to assist with technical issues, and how to reach you

Assist with feature overview as needed

1

Chapter (5)

Prepare Facilitators and Producers

In this chapter, you will learn how to prepare facilitators to deliver live online training:

- Identify common roles in the virtual classroom.
- Review selection criteria for facilitators and producers.
- Outline preparation steps for facilitators.
- Master the art of online facilitation.

While a well-designed program is essential to the success of your virtual training classes, it's only half of the equation. The other half—equally as important—is excellent delivery. Combined together, interactive design and effective delivery create the overall positive learning experience for participants.

In one of my train-the-trainer classes, I ask my participants to work in groups to create a list of characteristics of the "best" and "worst" training classes they have ever attended. Under the "best" category, it's usually responses like "great facilitator," "got everyone involved," "relevant, practical information," "hands-on practice," "enthusiastic trainer," and so on. And under the "worst" category, the responses almost always include "boring trainer who just read from notes," "unprepared speaker," "no engagement," "just listened to lecture," and so on.

In this same exercise, I ask the groups to select which of their statements relate to the training class design, and which relate to the training class delivery. They have to group their responses into one of those two categories. Often, their choices split down the middle. Getting everyone involved, including relevant practical information, and hands-on practice are typically associated with the training class design. However, my participants often argue that those factors can also be attributed to the facilitator. It's the facilitator who brings the design to life. And so often, it's the facilitator who makes or breaks the class.

In this chapter, we will look closely at the facilitator's role—how to select them, prepare them, and set up facilitators for success. We will also answer the question, "What makes effective virtual training delivery?"

Roles in the Virtual Classroom

Facilitators

Whether you call them trainers, facilitators, instructors, or some other name, this role is the leader of the virtual training session. They manage the classroom, teach content to the learners, guide everyone through learning activities, and facilitate discussion among participants. They speak, listen, direct, plan, lead, encourage, observe, and guide—all of the necessary actions that it takes for learning to occur in a classroom.

Effective facilitators enhance the experience for everyone in a way that motivates participants to learn. They ask questions to provoke thinking. They present content in ways that are easily understood. They give instructions to complete learning exercises. They encourage participation from everyone. And they create a comfortable and safe learning environment where participants are free to explore and practice new skills. The facilitator's ability to help participants realize their learning potential is paramount to the success of any virtual class.

In essence, you can think about the facilitator as the conductor of an orchestra. A conductor leads the show, but the music is made by the band. A conductor enables the musicians to play beautiful music. In the same way, a facilitator leads the class, but the learning happens through participants. The facilitator enables the learning.

Producers

For the in-person classroom, one facilitator usually runs the event. However, in the virtual classroom, there is another role essential to success, the producer. The producer is a second person who joins the virtual class as a session leader. You might immediately be wondering, why two leaders? Isn't one enough? Let's look at what the producer role does, and then come back to this discussion about why a second leader is important to have during a virtual class. To begin, it's important to note that there are two types of producers: co-facilitators and technical experts.

What's in a Name?

My preferred term for this role is "facilitator," for several reasons. Most importantly, the name keeps a slight emphasis on the participants. The leader facilitates discussion and learning among the group.

Compare the word facilitator to "instructor;" although these terms can be used interchangeably, "instructor" implies teaching and imparting knowledge to the learners. While that task is certainly an important part of many training classes, it emphasizes the leader's role as expert teacher. Unless this is a deliberate choice to establish credibility with the audience, I prefer to use the word "facilitator."

By habit I also use the word "trainer" since it's common vernacular among training and development professionals. Yet when asked to choose between "facilitator" or "trainer," I'll choose "facilitator."

Co-Facilitator

A producer who takes an active role in facilitating the class would be called a co-facilitator. He or she might present small portions of the content, or truly have an equal share of the facilitation responsibilities. In addition to the training responsibilities, this person would take the lead role with any technology issues that arise. The facilitator and co-facilitator would plan in advance of the session exactly who will do what, and when they will do it.

Technical Expert

A technical expert producer stays behind the scenes of a virtual training class. They help participants get initially connected to the class, assisting with any challenges that arise. They run the technology of the software platform. They open poll questions, put participants into breakout groups, and assist with other classroom tools as needed. If technical challenges arise during the class, the producer handles them. For example, if a participant drops from the audio due to a technical issue, the producer will work with them via private chat to help them get back online. Or, if the facilitator accidentally loses Internet connectivity, the producer can keep the class moving along while the facilitator reconnects. In some cases, the participants never even know the producer exists because his or her work is entirely behind the scenes. Yet other times, the producer will speak up to offer instructions for using the tools or to help a participant who needs an extra touch.

One of the best ways I know to describe the technical expert producer role is to think about a producer on a radio talk show. The talk show producer sits behind a control panel to operate the technical workings of the show. They also take care of the switchboard for callers, help the talk show host stay on time, and handle any problems that occur during the show. It's very similar for a virtual class producer—they operate the technical details of the training class.

The level of technical involvement can vary from producer to producer and class to class. Some facilitators, myself included, like to handle at least some of the platform features during a session. Personally I like to move my own slides, highlight key words on screen, and provide assistance to participants when they need it. It's a best practice for the producer and facilitator to plan ahead of time how they will work together during a class. See the checklist at the end of this chapter for some guidelines.

Location

A frequently asked question is, "Is it necessary for the facilitator and producer to be in the same room as one another?" The answer is no. Usually the facilitator and producer are in separate rooms, and often separated by lengthy distances—different cities or even different countries.

One reason for the distance is that it's not necessary for them to be in the same location. They have the virtual class platform to facilitate, communicate, and work together. They may even connect through a secondary back channel, such as mobile device texting or an instant messenger program.

The other, and more important reason, is for contingency planning. Should the leader in one location have any technical or connectivity difficulties, then the leader in the other location can continue class until the issue is resolved.

Why Two Session Leaders?

As stated, the most effective virtual training classes have two session leaders—a facilitator and a producer. Here are several reasons why.

First, it allows the facilitator to facilitate. One huge advantage of having a technical expert producer run the software and manage technology issues is that it allows the facilitator to focus on the participants and their learning. The facilitator doesn't get distracted or bogged down in technical issues because the producer is able to handle them. The partnership and division of responsibility between producer and facilitator makes for a better participant experience.

Second, it allows the participant to focus on the learning. A producer assists participants with technology questions or concerns, which allows the participant to focus on the learning. Without a producer, a participant who has trouble logging into the session may give up. But with a producer, they have a helping hand who can guide them into the session. Without a producer, a participant who struggles to use the annotation tools might focus more on the tools than on the learning activity. But with a producer to help explain and privately assist, the participant can more easily get involved.

One of the producer's roles is to teach and encourage participants with the technology. The producer may assist silently through private chat or aloud by giving verbal instructions. There are even times during a session when a producer may reach out by email or telephone to a participant who is struggling to stay online. The key is that it's the producer who is taking care of these issues while the facilitator keeps the rest of the class going. If a producer is not part of the session, the facilitator would have to stop, pause, and work with the one or two participants who need extra help.

John Hall, Senior Vice President of Oracle University, has measured participant satisfaction in his organization's online classes and found that classes with producers consistently score two percentage points higher on participant satisfaction surveys than classes without. Having a producer on board makes for a better participant experience.

Third, having a producer creates a technical safety net for the class. If one of the leaders were to lose connectivity, the other could continue the session. There are countless stories of a facilitator dropping from a call and the producer continuing the session while the facilitator reconnects. Not long ago, I was facilitating a class when all of a sudden the power to my home office went out. My Internet router went down, and I lost all connections—visual and audio. While I had backup systems ready to go, and could quickly reconnect to the class, it took a few minutes for that to happen. In the meantime, my producer was able to jump into action and get the class into their next activity while I was getting back into the session. Without a producer, a solo facilitator takes a risk with every virtual class.

If—despite these advantages and reasons to invest—having a producer does not seem to be an option for you, then here are some solutions to consider:

- Have a partial producer, someone who joins the session for the first 10 to 15 minutes to help with the initial connectivity.

- Have a facilitator-in-training play the role of producer.

- Find someone in the organization who wants to learn more about technology and train him or her to be a producer.

- Ask your platform vendor about technical support services offered, to see if they would provide in-session producer support.

- Partner with your IT department when scheduling classes, asking them to provide a producer resource during virtual training classes.

- Create a producer job role in your training department, and have that person be your full-time producer for virtual training classes.

- Hire an external partner who will supply producers on a class-by-class contract basis.

This list is just a start to the many creative ideas you could come up with for finding a producer resource. Use your imagination and innovation to find a solution that works for your organization.

Finally, I won't deny that many virtual training classes occur around the world on a daily basis with just one facilitator at the helm. Many of my clients say that their company simply will not provide funding or support to have a co-facilitator or producer. I have personally facilitated sessions without producer support. So while it can be done, it is not a best practice. It detracts from the participant learning experience and isn't a recommended way to deliver virtual training. It's risky from a technical perspective, and it keeps the facilitator from fully focusing on the participant learning.

Selecting Facilitators and Producers

The first step to facilitator preparation is to select them carefully. The best classroom facilitators don't necessarily make the best virtual training facilitators. And not everyone has the skills or knowledge to be an excellent producer. What qualities and characteristics should you look for in facilitators and producers? Here are the skills needed for each role.

Facilitators

Effective virtual facilitators possess a unique blend of training, facilitation, and technology skills. They:

- apply adult learning principles to the virtual classroom
- are technology savvy (or willing to learn)
- can engage an unseen audience
- make learners feel comfortable with the technology and the virtual learning environment
- are able to multitask effectively
- have credibility with the content/material.

"Like the traditional classroom, when searching for a virtual facilitator I look for someone who will extend themself to make the 'room' their own. With limited time together in a virtual room, the ability to quickly convey a genuine energy is important. Like the classroom, things can go wrong in a virtual room, yet virtual has more time pressure. You can't pause and say 'talk amongst yourselves while I fix this...' Flexibility and the ability to appear calm under pressure are vital. Without participants being able to see you, your voice tone becomes increasing important. We all know we're following a guide, yet the ability to 'read' in a conversational manner keeps people engaged."

—Jim Wilcox, Regional Training Manager, AchieveGlobal

"Effective virtual trainers are prepared but also able to think on their feet. They have a vibrant voice and are able to build rapport with participants. They also have command of the virtual platform tools."

—Wendy Gates Corbett, Global Training Director

Producers

The most effective producers also possess a unique blend of skills and abilities. First and foremost, they need to be experts in technology. Not only do they need to know the virtual training platform inside and out, they also need to have a solid understanding of computer hardware and software in general. Other important qualities include:

- problem solving and troubleshooting skills

- remain calm under pressure

- able to juggle multiple things at once

- think quickly on their feet and take action as needed

- desire and willingness to keep learning.

"A producer should have a calm demeanor, technical competence, and be a proactive learner. They stay calm when technical challenges arise, and handle issues with grace and ease. When a question is asked, if they don't know the answer, then they are curious to find out and go research it. They should always be willing to learn more about the software, and to share that knowledge with facilitators and participants."

—Kassy LaBorie, Product Design Architect, Dale Carnegie Digital

---

Once the facilitators and producers have been selected, the next step is to prepare them for effective delivery. While the next section focuses specifically on the facilitator's role in preparing for and delivering an engaging class, keep in mind that much of the facilitator preparation and delivery can be applied to the producer role as well.

Facilitator Preparation

Once a facilitator has been identified (or in some cases, self-selected) to deliver live online learning, the preparation begins. The good news is that if the person has any classroom training experience at all, it will be more of an upgrade than a brand new start. It's like learning how to drive a truck if you already know how to drive a car. There are some significant differences, yet the basic rules of the road are the same.

When you think about facilitator preparation, consider how an Olympic athlete prepares for the games. The athlete goes to extreme measures to get ready for their main event. Through disciplined measures of diet, exercise, practice, and sport-specific routines, they prepare themselves to win a medal and stand upon the podium.

In the same way, effective virtual trainers prepare relentlessly for live online events. Some may even think they go to extreme measures to ensure success. However, the saying, "proper preparation prevents poor performance," is just as true in the virtual classroom as it is in the athletic arena.

To effectively deliver virtual classes, facilitators need to learn:

- the basics of live online delivery

- the technology that will be used for delivery

- the content and design of the class.

On top of these three items, facilitators also need to learn how to develop contingency plans in case of technology problems or other unexpected challenges.

Learning the Basics of Online Delivery

Some organizations have formal train-the-trainer programs for virtual facilitators, to help them learn the nuances of delivering online. Others will pair a new facilitator with a more experienced facilitator to learn the ropes.

When Darlene Christopher, Knowledge and Learning Officer at the World Bank, identifies new virtual facilitators, she works with them individually on how they will deal with no visual cues from the audience. She uses a fantastic technique to help them get comfortable with an unseen audience. Before they even go into the online classroom, she will get on the telephone with them, have them ask a question and then have them mute their phone lines and count to ten. This simple practice helps the new facilitator get used to a few seconds of silence before anyone responds, which can be typical in a virtual class.

Important Point

The key element in preparing trainers is giving them enough time to learn the technology and enough practice to get comfortable engaging participants in the virtual classroom.

In a more formalized train-the-trainer program, Yum! University holds a "boot camp" for virtual facilitators. Each train-the-trainer participant completes three

20-minute self-paced e-learning modules: *leading virtually, content development,* and *platform basics.* Next, participants apply what they have just learned by creating a short virtual lesson. They then attend a two-hour virtual class with a small group to practice their short virtual lesson and receive feedback from others. Upon finishing the program, each participant gets an account on the online platform in order to continue practicing. They also have access to an internal site with additional tools, job aids, and a forum for asking questions.

Scheduling Facilitators: How Many Sessions per Day?

A frequently asked question is, "How many virtual classes can a facilitator deliver in one day?" There are several ways to answer this question. From a timing perspective, a facilitator should log into a virtual class approximately 45 minutes prior to the start time,* and needs between 15 and 30 minutes at the end to 'clean up' the room and finish class. This means for a 90-minute virtual class, the facilitator should have close to three hours blocked on their calendar. This amount of time translates into two or three virtual classes in a day if they are scheduled back to back. This timing obviously varies with class length. Also, remember that a break in-between sessions is recommended.

From a workload perspective, a facilitator can handle as many classes in a day as his or her stamina allows. Delivering a virtual class well requires enthusiasm and energy. For some facilitators, draining from this internal reservoir too heavily can lead to fatigue and loss of alertness, which will in turn have a detrimental effect on their ability to effectively deliver a virtual class.

*Some platforms allow for set up in advance of the session, while setup in other platforms has to happen at the beginning of the session. If the virtual classroom and all of its activities can be set up prior to the day of class, then logging in 30 minutes before start time is probably fine. If the virtual classroom has to be set up from scratch at the start of the session, then it's better to log in closer to 60 minutes in advance. I recommend 45 minutes as an average option.

Learning the Technology

The second part of preparing facilitators for a virtual class is all about the technology. Effective virtual facilitators are masters of the virtual platform. This means that they know the software and its features in-depth. They know what every menu command means and what every button does. They know how the program works from the host or presenter view, and they know how it works from the participant view. They are able to use all of the tools available and help participants use them as well. Effective virtual facilitators don't stumble around trying to find a command, but instead move with ease from one virtual tool to the next.

How do virtual facilitators learn the software platform? Mostly through practice, by clicking on every button and trying everything out. They set up virtual sessions with multiple computers and practice using the tools from both the presenter and participant views. They may also attend formal training offered by the software vendor to help learn the platform. And they learn tips from other facilitators by sharing ideas and resources online. The bottom line is that it takes time, play, and practice with the technology to learn it.

You might be wondering how long it takes to learn a platform. That's like asking how long it takes to learn how to ride a bike or drive a vehicle. It varies from person to person, depending upon their prior knowledge, confidence in themselves, whether they learn on their own or someone works with them, and how much practice time they put in. It's nearly impossible to put an exact number on the amount of time it will take.

Technology Resources Needed

While we are on the topic of technology preparation, let's explore the technology resources needed by facilitators. In chapter 3, we explored the general technology needed for virtual training. Let's return to this discussion from the perspective of facilitator setup. It's important for the facilitator to have the resources they need to deliver properly.

The first and most important thing a virtual facilitator needs is a computer from which to deliver the training class. It could be a desktop computer or laptop, provided that it is powerful enough to run the full (not mobile) version of the virtual class platform. It needs a reliable Internet connection—preferably wired instead of wireless. Even though most wireless connections are dependable, when delivering a live online class it's better to err on the side of caution. If there is any chance the wireless could be spotty or could have interference, then that's the reason to use a wired Internet connection.

The next thing a virtual facilitator should have is a second computer. Again, it could be a desktop computer or laptop, provided it can run the software and has a solid Internet connection. This second computer has a dual purpose. First and most importantly, so the facilitator can log into the virtual classroom as a participant and see what they see during the class. Since most virtual class platforms have a different view for facilitators and participants, having a computer logged in as a participant helps the facilitator guide and direct the class in a way that makes sense to participants. For example, if a class activity calls for participants to annotate on a specific part of the screen, the facilitator can give exact instructions to complete the activity—including exactly where to find a button—in a way that participants will easily understand.

This came in handy for me during one of my recent classes. I had given instructions for a whiteboard activity but the participants didn't seem to be following along because no one started typing on screen. Just before one of the participants spoke up to say they didn't have the typing tools, I glanced at my own participant computer, and realized that my producer and I had neglected to make available the participant drawing tools—we had hidden them after a previous activity. A quick click of the button fixed the situation and this new whiteboard activity began right away.

The second purpose of the facilitator's second computer is so that they can have a backup connection to the class in case of emergency. If their first computer was to crash or have some other problem, the facilitator would still have a way to communicate with participants and could continue delivering the session from this second computer. Depending on which software platform was in use, the producer could either promote this computer to be host with full facilitator privileges or the facilitator could "reclaim" the host role using a special code that was generated when the class was set up. Either way, this second computer serves as a safety net for the facilitator. A facilitator who operates without one runs the risk of disrupting a virtual class if an unexpected technology problem occurs.

In a pinch, this second computer could be a mobile device. I don't recommend facilitating from a mobile device, simply because at the time of this writing, the mobile device versions of most virtual classroom platforms are limited in their features and a facilitator needs the full functionality. However, a mobile device connection as a second computer is better than nothing, and if it's the only option available then a facilitator should use it as a second connection. In fact, when I am facilitating online, I actually like to have a mobile device connected to the session in addition to my second computer. That way, if any of my participants connect via tablet or smartphone, I know what they see on screen. It also gives me one more contingency option in case it's needed during a class.

Finally, a facilitator should also have a quality hands-free wired headset for use with their audio connection, whether they use a telephone or VoIP. The headset allows them to easily type and talk at the same time. The headset also gives a crystal clear connection, unlike a speakerphone which often has an undesirable echo which affects sound quality. Speakerphones also pick up extraneous noises such as shuffling paper, which would be distracting during class. A wired headset has the best sound quality for facilitators.

To give you a visual idea of a facilitator setup, here is a photo of what my desk looks like when delivering a virtual class:

Figure 5-1 My Facilitator Setup

On top of this standard technology setup, virtual facilitators must be prepared for contingencies and unusual situations. Since virtual classes rely on technology and the Internet, they create redundancies and backup plans as a "just in case."

Usually virtual classroom platforms function normally, and usually Internet connections are strong and steady. With a reliable platform, you might never expect anything to go wrong during a virtual class. However, that's exactly the reason it's important for virtual facilitators to prepare for the unexpected. By taking the extra step to think about and prepare a back-up plan, any unforeseen challenges will just be a temporary nuisance. For example, if the facilitator works from home and the Internet connection was to unexpectedly go down during a session, what could he do to reconnect? A facilitator would have thought about this contingency ahead of time and had a backup plan. Or, what if the facilitator's headset loses battery power during a virtual class? He should have a second headset readily available to switch, or a mobile phone nearby that could be used.

Backup plans could include:

- Know where the nearest public Internet connection is, and having a quick way to get there (such as walking across the street to your neighbor's house, or driving down the road to a coffee shop with free Wi-Fi).

- Have a backup Internet connection device, such as a mobile device with a data plan that could be tethered to the facilitator's computer.

By taking just a few extra steps to plan technology backups, an effective virtual facilitator will always be prepared.

Learning the Class Content

Finally, facilitators need to realize that in one respect preparing for a virtual class is no different than preparing to facilitate any instructor-led class. It's important to learn the class content and the design. Some facilitators will read through the guide several times, some like to observe the class as a participant, while others will practice facilitating to an "empty" virtual classroom. Regardless of the method, the facilitator should be a content expert prior to delivery.

In addition to mastering the content and class design, virtual facilitators should also get to know the audience. They should find out the answers to questions such as:

- Who are the participants? What are their names, roles, locations and other relevant demographic information?

- Do the participants know one another or are they meeting for the first time? If they know one another, what's their relationship? (For example, manager/employee, peers, other?)

- What's the reason they are taking this class? What do they hope to gain from it?

- What are their experience levels? Will the content be brand new information? Or are they knowledgeable enough to be teaching the course? Or somewhere in between?

- What types of questions might they have about the material? What concerns will they have? What challenges will they have in applying the content?

Again, the amount of time needed for facilitator content preparation will vary depending upon several factors: previous familiarity, complexity of topic, and quality of the facilitator materials. For a general guideline, in his 1985 book, Dugan Laird reported a U.S. Civil Service estimate that the ratio for trainer preparation time is 3:1 (three days of preparation for one day of class time). While this number is only an estimate, it gives a starting point for scheduling facilitator prep time to learn the content. Additional time should be granted to learn the technology platform, if needed. With new virtual facilitators, I would be generous and allow as much time as possible for them to feel comfortable delivering online.

Ongoing Preparation and Development

Once a virtual facilitator learns how to effectively deliver online, it's important for him to continue learning and continue practicing. The more he spends time in the online classroom, the better he will be. The facilitator who delivers every day or every week will a much better facilitator than one who delivers only once every few months. Also, it's good for the facilitator to receive periodic feedback in order to improve his skills.

To help a facilitator receive feedback, Peggy Page, Design Group Manager at TD Bank, uses a facilitator observation form called a "Facilitator Rubric." It measures both technical proficiency and facilitation skills and rates on a three-point scale (1 = not proficient, 2 = developing, 3 = mastery). The purpose of this form is to help a facilitator improve their delivery skills.

Figure 5-2 TD University Facilitator Rubric

Technical Skills	1 – Not proficient	2 – Developing	3 - Mastery
6. Use white board functions	Cannot enable or use basic whiteboard or whiteboard overlay drawing tools (text tools, highlighting, shapes, etc) or explain them to participants. Unable to clear whiteboard.	Can enable and use basic whiteboard or whiteboard overlay drawing tools (text tools, highlighting, shapes, etc) and explain them to participants. Able to clear whiteboard or selected objects on whiteboard.	Can use and explain all functions of whiteboard or whiteboard overlay, including advanced functions (select tool, change text, etc).
7. Use pointers	Unable to use pointer or explain pointer use to presenters; leaves pointer visible when not in use; unfamiliar with Host Cursors.	Able to use pointer and explain pointer use to presenters; turns off pointer when not in use; able to enable or disable Host Cursors.	Able to use pointer to enhance engagement; able to explain pointer use to presenters; turns off pointer when not in use; able to enable or disable Host Cursors.
8. Use polls	Unable to launch prepared polls; unable to control broadcast of poll results; unable to move or hide polls.	Able to launch prepared polls; able to control broadcast of poll results; able to move and hide polls.	Able to launch prepared polls easily; able to control broadcast of poll results; able to move and hide polls; able to create new polls as needed; able to open and close polls.
9. Use web cam	Unable to use web cam easily; cannot enable web cam for participants; does not present a professional image with web cam (clear, well-lit, etc).	Uses web cam well; uses web cam when a video pod exists in room but may not know how to launch a new video pod; looks directly into web cam and presents a professional appearance; able to enable web cams for participants.	Uses web cam well; looks directly into web cam and presents a professional appearance; able to "freeze" web cam view for stills; able to enable web cams for participants; able to launch a new video when needed or launch a hidden pod.
10. Manage layouts	Unable to locate or readily move to various layouts	Able to locate and readily move to various layouts	Able to locate and readily move to various layouts; can create new layouts or rename layouts
11. Manage Breakout	Unfamiliar with	Familiar with breakout	Masters breakout room

The Art of Online Facilitation

Once a facilitator is fully prepared, the next step is to actually deliver the class. Effective delivery is more than just presenting content from a set of slides. Just because a facilitator says it doesn't mean participants learn it. Also, as we learned in the previous chapter, ideally the virtual class is designed with high interactivity and a focus on participants. However, even if it is not, an effective virtual facilitator will create interactivity using the techniques described in this section.

So what are all of the techniques that virtual facilitators use to engage participants in the learning? They:

- build rapport

- create community

- read nonverbal body language

- set expectations

- use platform tools

- share only relevant examples

- use voice

- multitask effectively

- manage technology.

Let's explore each one.

Build Rapport

Think about someone you've talked with on the telephone but never met in person. Can you build rapport with them? Of course you can! It's similar in the live online classroom.

One way to build rapport in the live online classroom is to listen carefully to what participants say and incorporate their thoughts and ideas into the class. When participants feel heard and listened to, they are more likely to feel comfortable and connected to the facilitator and to the class.

For example, when greeting participants at the beginning of a class, I'll make a point to find out something about them and their experience with the training topic. Then, during the session, I will refer back to relevant details that were shared. It helps create a connection and helps them realize they have been heard. It builds rapport.

Justin Patton, a virtual facilitator with Yum! Brands, begins building rapport even before the class begins. He will send a message to participants in advance of the class, asking them to briefly respond with a short answer. He may ask, "Tell me one word that defines your coaching style" or "What's one tip you would share with someone about using email?" For those who respond, Justin incorporates their answers into the class.

Another way to build rapport is to say participant names. Have you ever heard your name mentioned from across the room? Your ears perk up and you become a little more interested in that part of the conversation. It happens in the virtual classroom as well!

Effective virtual facilitators use participant names frequently and with sincerity. They acknowledge people by name as much as possible (such as, "Julio, thanks for adding your thoughts to the chat. You've got a great point."). And they make connections between the content and participant comments ("Earlier, Sophia asked about challenges using this technique. Here's one solution that can be used."). They also incorporate participant names into examples, such as saying "So if Melissa was a manager, then…" When participants hear their own names during a session, they pay closer attention and it helps build rapport among the group.

Call on Participants by Name?

Some facilitators have been taught not to directly call on participants by name because this can create an uncomfortable learning environment by putting people "on the spot." The solution to this dilemma is an easy fix. Facilitators can use direct questions on occasion during a virtual class by using these three guidelines:

- Let participants know at the beginning of class to expect direct questions.
- Ask direct questions that do not have one single correct answer. (For example, instead of asking "Adam, what's the next step in the process?" you might ask "Adam, what thoughts do you have about this process?")
- Take turns with the direct questions. (For example, "I'd like to hear from at least three of you on this next question. Let's start with Emma first, and then Jose.")

The goal of calling on participants by name is to encourage participation, not to put someone on the spot or embarrass them. If you use this technique, use it only in a way that maintains a comfortable and safe learning environment.

Create Community

Speaking of connection, when geographically dispersed participants join a session, they are isolated from the group and often—even if subconsciously—feel alone. The facilitator needs to make special effort to draw the participants together into a community, so that they feel a part of a shared collective experience. When participants become part of a connected community, even briefly during a short virtual session, they will have a better learning experience.

In addition to a better learning experience, research shows that connected participants learn more and have higher satisfaction rates. In a recent study by Manuel Cebrian at the University of California San Diego, he analyzed 80,000 interactions between 290 students in a collaborative learning environment and found that the more a student interacted with other students, the higher they scored in the course (Jacobs School of Engineering, 2013). In addition, researchers at the University of North Carolina-Wilmington examined interactivity in the virtual classroom, including learner-to-learner interactions. Their findings concluded that "interaction is crucial to student satisfaction in online courses" (Martin, Parker, and Deale, 2012).

There are several ways a facilitator can create community. From a simple poll question that asks participants to share their common experiences, to putting participants in pairs or trios to discuss a topic, any time the facilitator connects participants to one another they are creating community. The facilitator is helping participants realize they are together in the experience, and helping them relate to one another. These participant one-on-one conversations can happen through a private paired chat activity or in small group breakout rooms. The more the facilitator creates the environment for this networking to happen, the better the class will be.

Read Nonverbal Body Language

It's a common misperception that a facilitator doesn't "see" participants in a virtual classroom. While it's true that participants and facilitators don't physically make eye contact with each other in the same way they do in a traditional classroom, it's false to believe that a facilitator doesn't "see" what goes on.

When I was a child, I used to think my parents had eyes in the back of their heads because they always seemed to know when I was doing something I wasn't supposed to. In fact, one time I distinctly remembering my father telling me that I couldn't have a cookie before dinner, but I went and got one out of the cookie jar anyway. And somehow he knew, even though he wasn't in the kitchen with me. In some ways, a virtual facilitator's ability to read the audience is just like my father's knowledge that I was eating the forbidden cookie. He just knew, because the evidence gave it away. And a skilled and experienced facilitator just knows when participants are paying attention and engaged in the class, or if they have drifted off to somewhere else.

The tangible ways a facilitator can tell if a participant is engaged include the chat window, poll question answers, verbal responses, and other learning activities. The facilitator knows who is connected and who is not. The intangible ways a facilitator can tell which participants are engaged is a little more difficult to explain. If the facilitator stays focused on the class participants and their learning, she will see who stays engaged and who disconnects literally (and figuratively).

Some virtual classroom platforms have an "attentiveness indicator" feature. This tool shows the facilitator which participants are attentive, and which are not, by placing a symbol next to their name when they click away from the web platform. While the theory behind this feature is great, it's imperfect because it relies on a participant's active window. Anytime a participant stays on the virtual classroom window, they are "attentive" and anytime they click to another window, they are "not attentive." Well, just because a participant's active window is the virtual classroom doesn't mean they are truly engaged. And they may click away from it to adjust the volume of their speakers, or they might be looking up something relevant to the learning, or even taking notes in a word processing software. So the attentiveness feature does not really measure participant engagement or learning. An engaged facilitator who is accutely tuned into participants is the best measure of a participant's level of engagement.

Set Expectations

Effective virtual facilitators strive to create a comfortable learning environment for participants. One way they do this is by setting expectations at the beginning of a session. They let learners know that the class will be interactive and their full participation is requested. They invite participants to get involved in the learning.

To help set expectations, a facilitator will:

- help the group establish ground rules at the beginning of class

- let participants know it will be an interactive class

- give specific instructions on how to engage (such as, "if you can answer 'yes' to this following question, please click on the 'raise hand' button" or "if you can answer 'yes' to this question, please type your name in the chat window").

This last point is important to remember, because there are so many options for interacting in the virtual classroom. If participants are confused about how to respond, they will probably remain silent instead of risking embarrassment. Virtual facilitators should set expectations appropriately.

Use Platform Tools

Effective virtual facilitators use all of the virtual classroom tools to their advantage. They frequently ask participants to respond by poll, chat, raising hands, and any other available feature. Facilitators help keep participants engaged by putting the tools to use. For example, when I am facilitating, I frequently ask participants to "give me a green check if you agree with this" or "add your thoughts to the chat window." While my facilitator guide is full of interactive exercises, I often insert these brief engaging techniques in addition to what's already written in the guide. I want to be sure that participants stay connected, and I make broad use of the platform tools to help me in this quest.

In Justin Patton's words, he asks himself, "How am I keeping them so busy that they don't have time to multitask?" because he knows that just a slide with words on it is not enough to keep the learners engaged. Justin wants to ensure his participants are learning and talking and participating in the session.

Share Only Relevant Examples

Another reason that participants stay engaged during a virtual class is that the content is relevant to their needs. If it's a skill they need to learn or a gap in their current knowledge, then they will be more apt to focus on the learning. Effective virtual facilitators can keep the class relevant by sharing stories and using examples that make sense in context.

For instance, if it's a class of experienced managers and directors, then any stories told by the facilitator should appeal to that population. If it's an audience of brand new interns who are just entering the workforce, then any shared examples should make sense to them. And, if it's a global class full of international participants, the facilitator should use culturally relevant analogies that everyone can understand.

Use Voice

Effective virtual facilitators make the most of their voice in order to connect with participants in the virtual classroom. Their voice should be engaging enough to keep participants attention during the entire session. Facilitators make the most of their voice's tone, volume, rate, and pitch.

According to a recent study, the ideal voice speaks around 164 words per minute, and pauses for 0.48 seconds between sentences. And at the end of a sentence, the tone should fall instead of rise (BBC News, 2008). In other words, a voice that falls at the end of a sentence sounds declarative, like the speaker is making a statement. But a voice that rises at the end of a sentence sounds uncertain, like the person is asking a question.

While not every voice matches this ideal, it's a good measure to strive for when seeking to improve delivery style. Virtual facilitators should have an energetic voice that conveys enthusiasm for the class topic. They want to sound confident and pleasant to the listening ear.

One way to measure the overall effectiveness of a facilitator's voice is to record a session and listen to the playback. Consider how it sounds to the ear. Does it capture your own interest? Is it clear and easy to hear? Is it too fast or too slow? Also, listen in for any extraneous filler words ("um," "ah," y'know," and so on).

Effective virtual facilitators will listen to their voices and make adjustments as necessary. They seek feedback and apply it to make the most of their voices.

Multitask Effectively

A skilled facilitator is like a duck gliding across a pond. An outside observer sees just smooth sailing on the water, yet underneath the duck is paddling furiously to propel itself forward. And like the paddling duck, an effective virtual facilitator juggles many tasks with ease. While most experts say that multitasking cannot be done well by anyone, it's a necessary skill for facilitating in the virtual classroom. There's a lot going on at once, and facilitators must pay attention to content, activities, timing, participant comments, and everything going on in the software platform. Effective multitasking comes from a combination of preparation and speed. Virtual facilitators who do it well are prepared, practiced, and proficient.

- **Prepared:** Effective virtual facilitators are prepared. One benefit of enough preparation time is how it contributes to effective multitasking. Effective multitaskers take time to prepare their workspace for a virtual class. They remove any unnecessary documents from their desktop, so that they can give sole attention to the screen. They have fully prepared for the class so they are not using extra energy to remember what comes next.

- **Practiced:** Effective virtual facilitators practice their craft. They practice interacting with all of the tools, and practice their facilitation techniques. Just like a world-class musician who plays a song over and over again until it sounds perfect, an effective virtual facilitator practices as much as possible to improve their skills. The more practice a facilitator gets with multitasking, the better they will be.

- **Proficient:** Effective virtual facilitators are proficient in what they do. By knowing the tools in-depth, they do not have to hunt for menu commands or stop to think about where to find something. They are skilled typists who do not need to hunt and peck at every key on the keyboard. This proficiency comes from practice, and leads to easier multitasking.

Manage Technology

Unforeseen challenges can occur during virtual classes—a participant may disconnect, an activity might not pan out as planned, or a distraction in the workspace might need to be addressed (such as a co-worker interruption or a barking dog in the audio background). Effective virtual facilitators expect one or more of these challenges to arise during class; it's part of the territory in virtual training. Handled gracefully, challenges are an opportunity for facilitators to stay calm, take care of the issue, and return their focus to the learning as quickly as possible.

Of course, effective facilitators who prepare relentlessly will be able to quickly rely on their backup plans for any unexpected technology challenges. If they lose Internet connectivity, they switch to their backup provider. If they disconnect from the audio, they quickly reconnect. If an activity doesn't work exactly as they had planned, they respond with flexibility and switch to something else. Their backup preparation pays off in these situations.

When it's a different type of challenge, one that occurs unexpectedly or one that would not be prevented with preparation, then an effective virtual facilitator will still respond with ease. When unforeseen challenges arise during a virtual class, a facilitator should do one or more of the following:

- Stay calm and take a deep breath.

- Let participants know what's going on (if appropriate).

- Use backup plans.

- Spend just a moment or two troubleshooting.

- Take a short break to deal with the situation.

Remember, it's the producer who is typically assigned the task of troubleshooting or handling any unexpected challenges that arise during class. That way, the facilitator stays focused on the participants and their learning while the producer works with the individual who needs extra care. However, the facilitator should also know how to manage technology challenges with grace and ease. If it's a situation that affects the entire class and it's not possible to continue, even with a producer working on it, then the facilitator should keep participants informed, take a short break if necessary, and regroup when possible. With a skilled producer, most challenges are temporary and can be easily overcome.

One Organization's Story

Dale Carnegie Digital has an extensive high-quality train-the-trainer process for new virtual facilitators. They begin with trainers who have already gone through the rigorous certification process to deliver Dale Carnegie content. In addition, potential virtual trainers have to be recommended by someone in their organization who can attest to their excellent delivery skills.

The virtual train-the-trainer process includes four live online sessions totaling 12 hours of learning time. Topics include how to facilitate online and how to engage participants in their own learning. The virtual trainer candidates then practice delivering using a "teach-back" methodology so they can receive feedback and coaching from a master trainer. The next step is to co-facilitate in tandem at least three classes totaling nine hours of delivery. They receive feedback and coaching on these co-facilitation sessions as well.

Once a virtual trainer has been endorsed to deliver online, they are required to attend refreshers each year to stay up to speed on both technology and content. The time, effort, and resources invested in Dale Carnegie's virtual facilitators lead to high-quality results.

In Summary: Key Points From Chapter 5

- Effective virtual facilitators create an environment that's conducive to participant learning.
- The most successful virtual classes have two session leaders: a facilitator and a producer.
- There are two types of producers: co-facilitators or technical experts.
- Successful virtual facilitators know the virtual classroom platform inside and out: every feature, tool, button, and command.
- Facilitators need sufficient technology resources in order to do their jobs well.
- The art of online facilitation includes nine techniques used by facilitators.

Checklist 5-1 Facilitator/Producer Preparation

Use this checklist prior to a session to help divide responsibilities between facilitators and producers.

- Review logistics and housekeeping to ensure consistency:
  - Date
  - Time
  - Time zone
  - Which platform? Which version?
  - Link to session
  - Host/administrative passwords
- Practice/dry run the class:
  - Discuss every activity and how it should work.
  - Confirm roles and responsibilities for platform features:
    - polls
    - whiteboards
    - chat
    - breakouts
    - other: _____
- Establish emergency protocols:
  - Determine backup communication channel (outside of platform).
  - Create backup and contingency plans.

Chapter 6

Prepare Participants

In this chapter, you will learn how to prepare participants to learn effectively in a live online environment:

- Recognize three reasons why participant preparation is a key to success.
- Help participants manage their own learning environments.
- Teach participants how to use the technology.
- Use change management techniques to help participants learn.

Implementing virtual training in your organization is more about changing hearts and minds about online learning than it is about adding new technology. This is because virtual training is just as new to participants as it is to many facilitators, designers, and managers. It's a significant change from the way they are used to learning in a traditional classroom. And therefore they need guidance and direction on how to do it well.

It doesn't matter if your participants are internal employees or external customers. In both cases, you will need to prepare them appropriately and set them up for virtual training success. Participants are participants, regardless of their organizational affiliation. So whether you are a training manager who only delivers learning to your own employees, or a vendor who provides virtual training to the general public, both situations call for preparing participants ahead of time.

When most organizations roll out virtual training, they usually focus on preparing content and facilitators, and thinking about the technology needed for implementation. Unfortunately, organizations often forget to consider the participants. If this important link is missed, a virtual training program will probably not meet all of the goals established for it. Participant preparation is a key ingredient to virtual training success.

Furthermore, for the organizations that do think about participants, it's often just to send a confirmation email message with the virtual class connection details.

While this approach may work for an online meeting, it's simply not enough for virtual training. Participants need to do more than just log in to the class at the appointed time. They need to do more than just show up. Even if your technology has been tested, and even if participants have the motivation to learn, there is still work to be done to prepare them.

This chapter will help you do just that—prepare participants to effectively learn in a live online environment. We'll start by looking at their typical experience and the reasons to place your focus on them. Then we'll explore three things to consider and do as you set up participants for success.

Focus on Participants

There are three main reasons to focus on participant preparation before virtual training:

- Virtual training is a **new way to learn** for most participants.

- There is a **shift of responsibility** from the traditional trainer to the participant.

- Participant **learning environments** are often not conducive to uninterrupted online learning.

New Way to Learn

Most adults have years of experience in a traditional classroom environment for learning. From a young age, they went to school, sat at a desk, and learned from a teacher. While this description doesn't fit everyone's experience, a large majority of adults can relate to formal learning in a school room.

Continuing into adulthood, most adults experienced traditional, formal corporate education programs that also took place in a classroom. They might have attended a two-day new hire orientation program offered at corporate headquarters, a one-day sales training workshop, a four-hour leadership program, or a crash course in how to use the newest company software program. Regardless of the topic, all of these programs probably took place in a traditional classroom with other learners and a facilitator.

When you think about the traditional classroom experience from the learner's perspective, some common features exist:

- The learner leaves her workspace to go to class. She might walk down the hall to a training room; or in some cases, she may have to leave home and travel overnight to the training location.

- While the learner may have a brief assignment to complete before arriving to class, most of the focus is on the classroom session—what will be learned during the session. For the most part, the learner only needs to show up to the room when the class begins.

- The classroom is a familiar place, even if the learner has never visited this particular facility before. Most classrooms have common features, such as the facilitator setup at the front of a room, a projector and screen for visual aids, and tables and chairs with a workbook and other necessary supplies (pens, sticky notes, and so on) readily available.

- Group social norms are established during class, either formally or informally. For example, the facilitator might lead the class in a ground rules discussion about being on time, and proper use of mobile devices during the session (usually to keep them on silent mode). The learner typically follows these rules during class to conform to the established social norms.

- The learner interacts with the facilitator and other participants through conversation, group dialogue, and structured activities.

In a virtual classroom, many of these traditions are left behind, leaving the participant in unknown territory for learning. For example:

- The learner stays at his workspace for virtual training.

- The learner is often expected to complete a pre-class assignment related to the training content.

- The learner has to figure out how to set up his computer and telephone in order to connect to the virtual session.

- The learner may or may not have experience with the specific virtual classroom platform used for this session, and therefore might see an unfamiliar screen upon logging in to the class.

- If the learner needs supplies—anything from a printed handout to a highlighter or sticky notes—then she most likely need to procure those items on her own. The learner has to print her own handouts, unless the virtual training coordinator shipped them a box with workbooks and supplies. However, shipping materials is not common for virtual training, it's more likely that participants will be expected to print a copy of electronic handouts.

- Group social norms in the virtual classroom may or may not be established, depending upon the facilitator's skill and the design of the class. Even if they are established, many learners find them to be optional because they believe they are invisible to others.

- In a well-designed virtual class, the learner will have opportunity to interact with the facilitator and other participants many times via the virtual class platform. However, many learners find that they are distracted by the environment around them and as a result choose not to fully engage with the class.

The bottom line is that virtual training is a new way to learn for many participants. From learning at their own desk space to the online platform setup, the differences can be uncomfortable for learners who are used to the traditional way of learning in a face-to-face classroom environment. Even participants who embrace online training still have an initial learning curve when getting started.

New Responsibilities

In addition to virtual training being a new way to learn for most participants, they also have a new set of responsibilities. They are expected to play a more active role before, during, and even after a virtual training session. Unless someone tells them about these new responsibilities, they won't know about them, and the success of your virtual training program will be compromised.

One of the most frequent complaints I hear from virtual facilitators is that their participants are not engaged in the session. In many cases, it's because the proper expectations have not been set appropriately with participants. Most participants think they just need to show up and listen, when in reality they are expected to do so much more.

For example, before the virtual training class, participants typically need to:

- Set up their computer, test their connection, and ensure appropriate software is downloaded.

- Complete an assignment of some type, intended to introduce them to the content.

- Create an appropriate learning environment—a place where they can concentrate and focus on the learning.

- Minimize distractions around them and focus on the virtual training class.

While these things might not seem like much, they can be a big deal to a participant who isn't used to doing any of the above. And if even one of the items is missed, it can lead to disaster.

For example, a participant who doesn't test his computer prior to the session might not be able to log in at the appointed time. Or the participant who doesn't complete the pre-class assignment might be lost during an activity. And the distracted participant isn't going to place full attention on the class and therefore will not be engaged in her learning. In addition, when the facilitator expects interaction, and a participant does not respond, then the rest of the class participants could be affected by missing out on a potentially valuable contribution.

Furthermore, during a virtual training class, there are additional expectations placed upon a participant. These expectations include:

- Connect to the class on time, or even a few minutes early.

- Use the platform tools, including chat, polling, drawing, and other interactions.

- Make connections with other participants during class activities.

- Actively participate in class discussions, responding to questions and contributing to the conversation.

These expectations are particularly difficult if participants have any experience attending a noninteractive webinar or webcast. These days, most participants have attended one of those, and therefore probably fall into this category. Based upon their experience as participants, they probably have a passive view of online learning and are not expecting to do anything during a virtual class. These participants tend to just show up, put their phone on mute, and continue to go about their work day while listening to the class as background noise. It's no wonder that the most common complaint I hear from virtual trainers is, "My participants are silent and don't engage!"

Therefore, educating participants on their new responsibilities, and making it easy for them to take on these responsibilities, are both important keys to success.

Learning Environments That Are Not Conducive

Perhaps the biggest challenge and change of them all is the fact that in virtual training, a learner has to manage her own learning environment. In a traditional classroom, it's the facilitator who creates the environment—in how they arrange the tables and chairs (u-shape, pods, chevron style, and so on), in what materials they place on each table (kinesthetic toys, supplies), to the ambiance, lighting, and posters on the walls. The participant walks into the room and immediately experiences whatever type of environment has been created by the trainer. But since participants don't leave their workspace to attend a virtual training class, this environmental component shifts to whatever happens to be in the participant's surroundings. The facilitator has much less influence in creating the learning environment during an online class than they do in an in-person environment.

Most participants in the middle of their daily workspace do not have a space that's appropriate for concentrating on learning something new. In fact, take a moment to look around at your own desk—would you agree? My own desk is currently cluttered with a myriad of folders, overflowing stacks of papers, beeping gadgets, and a pile of unfinished projects. I would find it hard to concentrate without clearing space.

It takes a good environment to listen and absorb new information, one that's conducive to learning. Participants have to be able to set aside distractions and focus to concentrate on learning a new skill. Even a clean desk doesn't solve the problem—a typical office worker is interrupted approximately every three minutes, either by their co-workers, by an electronic gadget, or by some other distraction (Silverman, 2012). And as John Medina points out, "studies show that a person who is interrupted takes 50 percent longer to accomplish a task. Not only that, he or she makes up to 50 percent more errors" (2008, 87). These distractions and interruptions in the learner's working environment can sabotage the success of your virtual training class.

Since learner environment challenges are so prevalent in most organizations, and they are an important consideration when setting your participants up for success, let's take a look at some typical workspaces that participants have to contend with.

Retail

Retail organizations have distributed workforces, which seem to be the ideal situation for virtual training. However, most retail store workers spend their time on the floor or behind a cash register. They spend time interacting with customers and merchandise, and are rarely behind a computer screen. Retail workers may have mobile devices for inventory lookup and customer transactions, but they actively use these devices to serve customers.

Most retail stores do not have a quiet place where workers can actively engage in a virtual training class. There may be a computer workstation that can be used for short asynchronous learning, but taking a 20- or 30-minute, self-paced class is not the same as actively engaging in a 90-minute, live online training class.

When I worked in a retail store many years ago, we had one tiny break room in the back of the store, with a small shared lunch table. There was also one shared manager office with a desk and computer, but neither of these places would have been a quiet place to learn due to the constant traffic flow and surrounding distractions.

Construction

Construction workers spend most of their time on a job site, and may or may not have computer access during typical working hours. When they do use computers, it's usually in the shared job site trailer that has been temporarily erected for office space. The shared space and construction site noise can make it difficult to concentrate in this environment. In addition, depending upon the site location, Internet connectivity may be a challenge.

When I worked in training management for a construction company, we would send an extra training laptop to job sites that could be placed in the trailer. It was for shared use by everyone at the site, and mostly used by supervisors who needed to take required self-paced e-learning courses. While it worked as a training solution, it was often a challenge to justify sending an extra laptop to the site. In addition, many employees found it a challenge to find time to step away from the job site and into the trailer, even for required training. And similar to the retail environment, a quiet space without interruption or distractions was difficult to find.

Cubicles and Shared Workspace

Many office environments maximize space by installing cubicles or having an open floor plan. Employees have limited privacy in these open workspaces, even when walls are erected between desks. Noise levels tend to be high in this environment, and abundant distractions exist. Without doors or other "do not disturb" features, interruptions can be frequent. Co-workers stop by, or conversations can be overheard.

At the last office building I worked in on a daily basis, my own cube was near a busy intersection in the office, and not far from a shared printer. Even when co-workers tried to be courteous and mindful about noise, I was frequently distracted by hallway conversations and loud equipment.

On the plus side of cubicle space, most workers will have their own computer and telephone line to participate in virtual training. However, the distractions could be a potential drawback and make for difficulty concentrating. In addition, one of my recent virtual training participants in a leadership class could not fully participate in the activities. He let me know through private chat that his team sat in the cubicle desks next to him and could hear his conversation. Therefore, he was not able to openly discuss leadership issues and coaching challenges along with the rest of the class. He missed out on the bulk of the learning experience due to his unsuitable environment.

On the Road

Millions of people work from locations other than their organization's office (Kalman, 2011). Salespeople, executives, and other traveling employees often find themselves in hotels, airports, and other public spaces during the workweek. Using portable laptops and public Wi-Fi, they connect to the Internet wherever they can find space. The common thread of these environments is the public nature and unknown experience that can be had.

Even in a hotel room, with a seemingly solid Internet connection, the ups and downs of shared Internet connectivity can wreak havoc on a virtual training session. Last month, I tried to participate in a virtual training class from a hotel room, and despite testing my connection ahead of time, I lost contact with the session twice during the hour. The experience was frustrating.

As a traveling speaker and trainer myself, I am intimately aware of the challenges of finding a quiet space to attend virtual training classes. I have tried airport executive lounges, rented hotel conference room space, and reserved back tables in public coffee shops, all in a quest to find a place to concentrate and learn while on the road. It's not easy, and takes deliberate planning. Even when I think I have found the perfect spot, it seems that something unexpected happens that gets in the way of my pre-planned quiet space to learn.

In addition, traveling employees may be more likely to join a virtual training session from a mobile device. While mobile devices are the future of personal computing, right now the mobile versions of most virtual training platforms have limited functionality for participants. They may not be able to answer a poll question, or participate in private chat, or annotate on a whiteboard. Until the mobile platforms are fully integrated with other platform connections, mobile participation remains a limited option. Participants who don't realize this fact will be at a disadvantage.

At Home

According to the 2010 U.S. Census Report, approximately 10 percent of the American workforce works from home at least one day per week, and almost 7 percent work from home exclusively. For some, this arrangement creates an ideal working environment because it eliminates workplace distractions. No co-workers stopping by to chat, no office noise, and no water cooler conversations.

While many people claim to be more productive at home, the eliminated office distractions are replaced by a whole new set of challenges. First, not everyone has a dedicated home office space. Many telecommuters work at their kitchen table or from the living room couch. These locations offer a myriad of potential distractions during a virtual training class, such as televisions or pending household chores. Second, even for those telecommuters who do have a dedicated workspace, the potential for general distractions—ringing doorbells, barking dogs, and children needing attention—remains high. Third, home Internet connectivity may or may not be reliable, and so extra care needs to be taken for technology setup.

One of my participants in a recent class had connected from home, and every time she spoke we heard loud background noises that decreased her sound quality. Her home wireless connection had significant interference that she didn't notice during regular use, but it affected her ability to participate in our virtual class. Another participant, in a different session, kept stepping away from the class while he tended to his barking dogs.

The Bottom Line

Even if we have the best class in the world, well designed and expertly facilitated, participants won't pay attention or learn if they are unable to focus on class due to an incompatible learning environment. If a participant has trouble connecting, staying connected, or staying engaged due to his surroundings, then he will not be able to learn. We must recognize the challenges that many participants face in creating an appropriate learning environment, and do what we can to set them up for success.

Three Ways to Prepare Participants

So if these are the reasons why we need to focus on participants, let's turn our attention to how to set up participants for success in virtual training. More specifically, there are three ways to help participants:

- Help them manage their learning environment.

- Help them learn technology.

- Help them change their mindset about virtual training.

Let's explore each one in more detail.

Help Them Manage Their Learning Environment

Since participants need a space that's conducive to learning, and many of them do not easily have access to this type of space, it's important to help participants manage their environment. There are several options for helping, let's review them so that you can choose the one that best suits your environment.

Create a Learning Space for Them

While it's tough to deny the convenience of staying at one's desk to attend a training class, if it's not the right place to learn or they don't have a desk, then create a space dedicated to virtual training participation. This space might be temporary, such as reserving a conference room for the participant to use during class. Or it could be more permanent, such as a small office reserved for virtual training participants. You might also ask a manager to give up their office for a few hours so that their employees can attend a virtual training class.

If your office simply does not have a good space for learning, allow for telecommuting on days when participants are scheduled for training. Even though the home office location may not be ideal, weigh it against the office location and help determine which one has the better environment for learning. Despite the distractions listed in the section above, with a few tweaks, the home location might be best.

This option of creating learning space is obviously easier if participants are employees of your own organization; however, if they are not, consider all options. If you have access to office space in the geographic locations of your external participants, consider inviting them to attend virtual training in this space. Or, recommend nearby locations that offer temporary or rental workspace. At minimum, take extra care to communicate the importance of creating a good learning space for virtual training.

Using Conference Rooms for Virtual Training

When multiple people from the same office location register for the same virtual training class, they often think it's convenient to congregate in a conference room to participate. They bring their laptops and then either try to connect individually via audio or use the shared conference room telephone line. Either way, this situation creates challenges for virtual training for the following reasons:

- Virtual training classes are designed for participants to be in dispersed locations, not together in the same room. Activities will run differently, even if participants have their own laptops and can individually respond to poll questions and type in the chat window. In some cases it's a subtle difference, such as participating in a paired chat exercise. Dispersed participants experience paired chat as a way to connect with other virtual participants, while those in the same room can just speak to the person sitting next to them. It's a small but subtle change to the virtual classroom dynamic. Participants who aren't in the same room will feel left out, even if it's not on purpose.

- In addition, activities that make use of audio, such as breakout groups, can be challenging when participants are together in the same room. First, the audio quality is often compromised with so many connections in the same room, and the potential for static feedback and sound interference is high. Second, the activity instructions need to be modified for participants in the same physical room, which can be confusing for everyone.

If you know that a group of participants will be sharing conference room space, then consider the following options:

- Hold an in-person class for the participants in the same location. There may be enough to warrant sending a facilitator to this location.

OR

- Design the session so that it accommodates this type of audience. Plan activities and facilitator instructions for groups in a conference room. Don't try to mix and match groups and individuals in the same class. If you do, it will create extra work for the facilitator and create an extra unwanted dynamic between the mixed group of participants.

Offer Tips for Organizing Their Own Space

Another option to help participants manage their environment is to offer tips for organizing their own workspace. Do this by communicating with participants prior to your virtual training event about how to set up and prepare for class. The communication can be via email, or if possible, even by telephone. A warm welcoming phone call from the facilitator to the participant can go a long way in establishing a relationship, setting the stage for an interactive virtual class, and offering useful information about what's expected for preparation.

If the pre-class communication is automated, such as a scripted registration email from a learning management system, then separate out the workspace preparation message from the class connection details. In other words, use two or three messages to communicate with participants prior to the class. One message could be a "welcome to the program," a second message could provide the workspace preparation information, and the third message the class details.

Regardless of how you convey the news, keep your communication short and easy. You don't want participants to feel like they have to fully reorganize their desk just to come to class. The message can be simple: "clear some writing space on your desk, have the necessary materials ready to go, and shut down all computer programs except for the virtual training platform." Or instruct them to follow a short checklist that includes both technology tips as well as workspace tips. (See the sample checklist at the end of this chapter for details.) If participants will be connecting from home or on the road, include tips for finding a space without distraction and with reliable Internet connectivity.

As part of your pre-class materials, send messages that will help participants deal with interruptions. Encourage them to turn off their telephone ringer and set aside their smart devices prior to class. Have them block their calendar, starting 15 minutes prior to the session and lasting five to 10 minutes after the session. Inform their managers (or ask participants to inform their managers) about the training class times so that, if needed, work coverage arrangements can be made. You can also include a "do not disturb" sign that participants can hang on their door or outside of their cubicle during class. Explain why these steps are recommended—it's so they will benefit from the interactive session and be able to fully engage in the learning. Remind them that they are participating in a training class, and not just dialing into a meeting or attending a passive presentation. You can be creative in sharing these tips. Instead of a standard email message, consider a catchy marketing slick. Or use a prerecorded voice message or text message reminders.

One fantastic idea comes from a large technology company that invites participants to watch a four-minute video prior to attending any virtual class. The video touches upon three topics—how to connect to the session, platform tools that will be used, and tips for effective learning. The tips include avoiding distractions, expectations for participation, and a reminder to avoid attending from non-conducive learning spaces.

Calendar Options

If you use a shared scheduling system to block time on someone's calendar for training, then block a few minutes before and after each virtual training session. In other words, if the session is scheduled from 3 p.m. to 4 p.m. ET, schedule the calendar meeting to begin at 2:50 p.m. and last until 4:05 p.m.

This "extra" time allows the participant to get set for the class and connect to the platform in time for the class to begin. It also allows for a few extra minutes at the end of a class for the participant to transfer notes and action items to their proper place before getting back to their work day.

The extra few minutes also gives the added benefit that participants won't think of the training class as just another meeting that they can sandwich in-between other meetings; but instead, that it is a training class with different expectations than just another appointment.

Start Each Virtual Class With an Accountability Check

Educating participants about creating a conducive learning environment starts before the class begins. But it is also a good idea to remind participants again at the start of each class, especially if any participants missed out on the pre-session communication. This "accountability check" helps participants get ready to learn. There are many ways you can remind participants to manage their environments as they log into the session.

First, use the opening screen of your virtual training platform (sometimes called a "lobby") to share workspace tips and reminders. Even if you have shared this information prior to the session, and even if you have repeat participants, it's always a good idea to remind them again.

Second, at the start of class (or just before the start time), run through a brief checklist of things to do to manage distractions. Make the checklist interactive by asking everyone to close out of email and then "raise their hand" when they have completed it. Or give them 30 seconds to eliminate one distracting thing from their desk and enter a note in the chat window when they return.

According to Treion Muller, Chief eLearning Architect at FranklinCovey, every one of their virtual classes begins with a 40-second etiquette video. It's a fun animated look at how to participate in an online class. It helps participants know what to expect, and reminds them to manage their environment so that they can participate. The idea is similar to an airplane safety video, except it focuses on participant expectations for the virtual class.

Another fantastic starting reminder comes from virtual training expert Karen Hyder, who posts a poll at the beginning of her virtual classes. The poll question asks participants to rate themselves on how engaged they plan to be during the session. The way the question and answers are worded calls immediate attention to the importance of learners managing their own distractions during class.

Give Grace When Needed

While we know that learner engagement in any training session, including virtual classes, is a key to success, there are times when it's equally as important to give grace. What does it mean to "give grace"? It means to extend courtesy and understanding to participants, to maintain a comfortable learning environment, and expect that participants have good intentions when joining the session.

If we come from a place of acceptance and understanding, expecting that participants have followed our instructions to create a good learning space, and treating them like educated adults who are responsible for their own learning, then we will be much more likely to receive respect and compliance in return.

Consider this scenario: A participant follows instructions and takes care to establish an appropriate learning environment and alert their co-workers "do not disturb" them during class. However, an unexpected emergency comes up during class and the participant has to step away from their screen for a few minutes. It's not intentional, it's not deliberate, and it's not because the participant doesn't value the importance of the session. It's simply an emergency that needs immediate care. The graceful response in this situation is to make a personal note of the participant's brief absence, and not make a big deal over it. If the participant missed a key learning point, or needs a moment to catch up, then the facilitator or producer can assist him with the next activity. It's essential to maintain a comfortable and welcoming learning environment instead of putting that participant on the spot and making an embarrassing example out of him.

It may be a different situation if the participant doesn't prepare, doesn't have intention of engaging with the class, and doesn't stay connected longer than a few minutes at a time. In that case, it would be very appropriate to have the participant reschedule the class to another time and place where they can focus. However, it's often easier to assume the worst instead of recognizing that most participants, if they have been educated, will make an effort to connect to class from a good place.

In Summary
While it seems simple, helping participants think through preparation can be the most important thing you can do to prepare learners. This small but super important detail is critical to virtual training success. Communicate that information to participants. Otherwise your participants will be distracted and most likely unengaged.

Help Them Learn Technology
The "tech-savviness" (or technical comfort level) of your participants may be a hurdle along the way to successful virtual training. Research has shown that the participants' technical knowledge and ability to use the virtual classroom tools have a direct impact on the quality of their learning experience (Falloon, 2011). While most people today know the basics of operating a computer, there are still varying

levels of proficiency among a typical workforce. And even if they are generally proficient in using a computer, they may not be familiar with the virtual platform. Here are a few specific items to ensure participants learn enough technology to be able to fully participate in the virtual training session.

Hardware

Find out if learners have what they need to connect to the session, and if they have the knowledge to use these items. For example, if you plan to play multimedia files, do the participant computers have sound cards? Do they know where to find the volume controls for adjusting the sound? How about headsets for their audio connection? Are they able to plug them in and adjust as needed? Do they have sufficient Internet bandwidth available? If not, do they have the ability to make changes to it? If they are expected to print a handout, do they have access to a printer? Will they be using personal computers or mobile devices? Are any of these items new, or are the participants experienced in using them?

In addition, what type of computers are the participants using? Do they use Macs or PCs? Will anyone try to connect using mobile devices? What extra setup might need to happen as a result of the learners' hardware choices? Hopefully, if you partnered with your IT department when planning ahead for virtual training in your organization, these items are already procured and in place. However, there are many occasions when it would be important to double check: when participants are external customers or not part of your organization, when participants are new and may not have been part of the technology review, or when participants are unknown to you in any way.

Headsets and Speakerphones

In order for participants to listen and speak during a virtual training class, they need a reliable audio connection. Whether it's a VoIP or telephone connection, they should have a headset for ease and convenience. It's uncomfortable and ergonomically incorrect for someone to cradle a phone to their ear for 60 or 90 minutes.

Unfortunately, a speakerphone is not the best solution in lieu of headsets. Not only does broadcasting audio disrupt the work of those around a participants, it often provides poor audio quality when the participant speaks. If the voice echoes or extra static is heard, it could potentially disrupt the virtual class.

Software

Find out if participants need to download any software to log in and participate, based upon the virtual training platform you have selected. For example, participants might need Flash, or Windows Media Player, or another add-in required by the virtual platform. If downloads are required, do participants have administrative rights on their computers? Or will they need special permission or assistance from the IT department? If they will use mobile devices to connect, find out what differences exist between the mobile software and the full web version of the software. (And, if the differences are great, then educate participants accordingly about the importance of not connecting via mobile device).

In addition, find out if participants have experience using the virtual training platform. There might be a range of experience, from novice to expert, but knowing ahead of time will help you choose the right solution for educating them about its features. And if participants need assistance and support, who should they call with challenges? The facilitator? The producer? Someone in IT? The virtual training platform vendor? There is not a right or wrong answer to this question, but it is one that you will want to address with participants and let them know that someone is available to help them.

"You've got to make virtual training easy for participants to do. You don't want them to struggle."

—**Lucy Brown, Senior Training Manager, IHS**

Five Ways to Help Participants Learn Technology

There are at least five ways to help participants learn technology in preparation for a virtual training session. Some of these methods have the added benefit of allowing you to educate participants on other topics as well, such as an overview of the technology and reminders to create an appropriate learning environment. The five techniques are as follows:

- **Hold a live online session designed to teach participants how to learn online.** Make this session a required prerequisite for attending any of your virtual classes. The session goals include gaining experience in how to connect to a session, a tour of the platform features along with learning how to use them, setting expectations for an interactive learning session, and tips for creating an appropriate learning environment. This session could be anywhere from 30 to 60 minutes depending upon the platform you use, which features you cover, and how many activities you decide to include. Many organizations hold these live sessions on a regular basis, and simply make them required prior to attending any virtual training class.

- **Create a self-paced asynchronous session that tours the virtual platform and provides preparation tips for participants.** This option is very similar to the one above, except that it will not actually replicate the connection experience for participants. If your organization does not have the resources to hold live online prerequisite sessions, or your learners would not be able to attend them, then this option may be the best choice.

- **Invite new participants to log in early for an overview of the virtual platform.** It would be important to distinguish between this overview session and the actual training class, so that both participants and facilitator have time to transition between. When choosing this option, ask new participants to join the session 30 minutes prior to the start time, and use approximately 15 to 20 of those minutes teaching the tools and setting expectations. The remainder of the allotted time becomes the transition to class, as regular participants will begin joining the session.

- **Teach the tools as needed during the session.** In lieu of the first option, a prerequisite live online session, this is the option I most frequently choose. While it does not address setting up the learning environment, it gives participants the instructions they need when they need them. For example, when it's time to use the chat window, take a moment to show a screen shot or point to the chat and explain where and how to type. Those participants who already know how to use it can begin the activity, and those who need the extra assistance will receive it.

- **Share a job aid or reference card with tips for using the technology.** This short document could be shared with participants ahead of time, either along with the handout or as a separate document. It could also be shared at the beginning of a session, using the virtual platform's file sharing feature. It should include screen shots of the virtual classroom platform, with very clear instructions on how to use the tools that will be required during class. Keep it both simple and useful, so that participants will easily be able to follow along.

Remember, your overall goal in teaching technology to participants is to make things simple and easy instead of hard and frustrating, so that participants have a good experience preparing for and attending a virtual training class. Use whichever one of these options makes the most sense for your learners and your virtual training classes. And of course, you could combine several of the options for best results.

"I spend a few minutes at the beginning of a virtual class to educate attendees about the features/buttons that I plan to use (chat, voting, annotation, etc.)."

—Jeff Robinson, Global Talent Management, Covance Laboratories

---

Tech Checks

One of my clients was getting ready to roll out a 10-month blended learning curriculum, which included 12 virtual training sessions spread over time. Most of the participants were brand new to virtual training, and would be joining the sessions from home.

To help prepare each participant, for both the technology needed and to educate them on creating an appropriate learning environment, we scheduled several "tech check" sessions prior to the program start date. Participants were able to choose which session they attended; however, attendance at one was mandatory.

Each tech check lasted 30 minutes and included the following:

- Log in to the system using the computer they planned to use during the training to test their connection and to learn how to dial into the audio connection.
- Take a tour of the virtual training platform features, by having them complete several introductory activities using the tools.
- Provide an overview of the blended curriculum, answering any questions they had.

By holding these mandatory tech check sessions, the first class was able to begin right away without any technology hiccups or participant issues.

Help Them Change Their Mindset

As said earlier in this chapter, implementing successful virtual training is often more about changing attitudes and beliefs than it is about adopting new technology. Of course the technology is also important; to be successful with this new way of learning, you must recognize the critical role that change management will play.

While a full discussion of change management goes beyond the scope of this book, let's look at four specific proven techniques that can be used to help participants eagerly adopt virtual training as a way to learn.

"Think about change management that goes along with a virtual training rollout. Be mindful from the very beginning about the impact that virtual training will have on your participants."

—Erin Laughlin, Senior Director Global Learning Delivery,
Marriott International

Here are four specific techniques to help change participants' mindsets about virtual training:

- Start small, then expand.

- Gain manager support.

- Anticipate questions and concerns.

- Communicate early and often.

Start Small, Then Expand

If this is your organization's first venture into virtual training, start small and then expand. Run a pilot on a simple topic that you know will be wildly successful. Invite a small group of participants who are eager to learn. You can select this small group from a business unit that is struggling with a specific business issue, and use the virtual training class to provide a solution to it. Or, hand select a team of individuals who you know will be supportive and willing to try something new. Or, ask for volunteers so that your first group of participants consists of those who have chosen to join in.

By focusing on a small group of "early adopters" and those who want to learn this way, you will be much more likely to have initial small victories that lead to even larger success. A few quick wins with virtual training will help build momentum toward larger ones. When participants hear news of a successful initiative, they will probably be more open to it.

By the way, if you have already adopted virtual training in your organization but have realized that you need to go back and make changes, or you need to revise what you have been doing to make improvements, then do the same thing. Start small, with the "new" way of learning, and apply the techniques learned in this book. Consider a rebranding effort. Use a different name, a different logo, a different group of participants. Once you start to see successes in this small area, then increase and expand your efforts.

Gain Manager Support

If you're asking participants to do something new, like adopt virtual training, it's important to educate and involve their managers. Not only do participants need the support of their direct supervisor in order to fully participate in a virtual training program, participants need support before and after the event as well. Research shows that the manager's role before and after an event are critical factors to successful learning transfer (Broad and Newstrom, 1992).

I experienced this truth several years ago when I delivered two half-day, in-person leadership classes for an organization. The morning group showed up for the class on time, prepared, eager to learn, and ready to participate. We had plentiful discussion and participants actively planned how to apply the content to their own situations. However, in stark contrast, the afternoon group was exactly the opposite. Several showed up late, most were not prepared, and participation was sparse. After the class, I learned that the manager of the morning group had used time during a team meeting to talk about the upcoming training and its importance. He mentioned that they would talk about it again at the next team meeting. Yet the manager of the afternoon group said nothing at all about the training to his group. They had only received an email notice informing them of the training date, with very little detail or explanation, and no mention of expectations.

I believe that the managers' approaches with each group made the difference in each training program's success. And more importantly, in what each group learned and was able to apply afterward. While this situation happened in an in-person class, it could have just as easily happened during a virtual training event. The participants' managers—and their buy-in to the training—have direct influence over its success. Therefore, not only is it important for you to prepare participants for virtual training, it's equally essential for you to gain support from their managers.

In addition to needing a managers' support of the training topic, you need their support for the training modality. For example, if a manager is not aware of a virtual training, then they may see an employee sitting at their desk looking at a website, and interrupt them to ask a question, not realizing they are participating in a training class. Or they might think the employee is just surfing the web without anything better to do at that moment.

Educate managers on virtual training—what it is and what they can expect. You could include managers in your initial implementation team (as discussed in chapter 2). You can also involve managers in the learning in the following ways:

- Invite managers to attend a kickoff session.

- Create a special communication piece for managers to explain virtual training.

- Provide a "manager guide" to the virtual training class (see the sidebar for an example).

- Have a participant assignment for them to talk with their manager prior to attending the session.

"We get the participants' managers involved with setting up a workstation for new employees to join our virtual training classes. We send a checklist with instructions on how to set up a quiet space conducive to learning. This checklist also includes technical requirements, such as a wired connection, their own phone, and a headset to use for audio during training."

—**Lisa Brodeth Carrick, Executive Director, Comcast University**

Anticipate Questions and Concerns

Questions and concerns accompany all changes. By thinking through what questions participants will ask about virtual training, you can anticipate and proactively respond before the questions turn into concerns that create challenges for a successful rollout.

For example, some participants may wonder if all training will now be conducted virtually. While other participants, who enjoy traveling to attend in-person training classes, might be concerned that their opportunities to visit with remote colleagues will be limited. And still other participants will have questions and concerns about the technology used for virtual training. These types of questions and concerns are normal parts of any change initiative. Even if participants (and future participants) stay silent, the questions may be under the surface.

When you take the time to plan ahead and anticipate questions, you can quell any misperceptions about virtual training before they begin. You can also take initiative to share correct information about the virtual training. The more information participants have, the less they will fear this new way of learning and the changes it may bring.

Creating a Manager's Guide

I designed a blended learning leadership curriculum for first-line managers of a global organization. The program included eight virtual sessions over a period of six months, plus self-paced assignments in-between. To effectively prepare participants for the full commitment and to help them maintain momentum, we decided to involve their managers.

First, I invited the participants' managers to attend the first "overview" session. This kickoff session explained the learning objectives, the training schedule, and the time commitment involved. It also reviewed "what is virtual training" and the importance of participant interaction and engagement throughout the curriculum.

Second, I created a "manager's guide" to correspond to the training curriculum. This guide included:

- program topics and learning outcomes
- program schedules, including exact times of all virtual sessions and the time commitment expected from each participant
- a topic-related discussion question (or two) to ask participants at set times during the curriculum
- tips for supporting participants' in their learning (such as allowing time for learning and participation).

I sent the document electronically to each manager, then invited them to print it and refer to it often throughout the curriculum as a guide to help their participants.

Communicate Early and Often

Speaking of sharing information, the more you communicate with participants prior to virtual training, the better. We talked earlier in the chapter about pre-session communication, and I'll address the specifics of communicating logistics in the next chapter. The point here is to use these communication opportunities to help participants have the right mindset and be successful in virtual training.

For example, if you know participants in an upcoming training class will be brand new, then an extra phone call from the facilitator would be a nice touch. Or a personalized email message, addressed to each individual participant, can help build rapport between facilitator and learner. Use these opportunities to set expectations, answer questions, and explain what the virtual session will be like. Also, consider your communication opportunities after the session. You can thank participants for engaging in their own learning. A brief thank you goes a long way and helps participants feel valued.

Participant Troubleshooting Guide

Here are some of the most common participant challenges that surface, and ideas to overcome them.

#1: Participants don't complete their pre-work.

If participants don't complete a pre-work assignment, it's usually for one of two reasons. Either they didn't know they needed to do it, or they didn't think it was important enough to make time for it.

There are two solutions for this challenge. First, don't call it pre-work. Be mindful of the assignment name. Call it something that indicates weighty importance—pre-work sounds unimportant and uninteresting. Choose a catchy name that works in your organizational culture, such as "action assignment" or "the three-step setup." Second, make it as easy as possible for them to complete. Let them know exactly how long it should take, give them all the necessary resources they need, and make the instructions easy to find.

#2: Participants don't engage during a virtual session.

This is the single most common challenge I hear from online facilitators. They say, "My participants are silent. I ask a question and no one responds." Or they complain that participants are multitasking and checking email during a session instead of paying attention to the learning.

The solution for this goes back to setting proper expectations with participants before the session, and having an effectively designed virtual training program with frequent interaction. If you follow the recommendations in this book, your participants will be much more likely to be engaged in their own learning! For example, if the design calls for 15 minutes of lecture about how to use the platform and an overview of the class agenda, and then the facilitator asks the first question, of course there will be silence. As discussed in chapter 4, creating a great opening is one way to engage participants from the start. This is just one of many techniques you can use to set the stage for interaction and engagement.

#3: Participants don't like virtual training.

Remember that most participants have experienced only lecture-style webcasts, and equate that to virtual training. And very few adults like to be lectured to! Or, if participants have attended virtual training, then it's possible that they did not have a good experience either due to course design issues, lack of facilitator skills, or technical challenges. Therefore, your goal in this situation is to create a fantastic learning experience for participants.

To create this type of experience, design an interactive session and use a skilled facilitator. Remember adult learning principles and apply them to class. For example, most people don't like to be told what to do, and prefer to make choices over what they do and when. Therefore, give participants a choice of when to sign up for virtual class instead of assigning them to a session. Also, make it relevant to them. Give them choice of discussion topics in class. For instance, you might have a breakout group activity where they will discuss challenges of implementing a new system. Instead of you pre-assigning the top challenges, allow time for participants to share their perceived challenges and then have the group vote on their top three. Use those top three choices for the breakout group activity. This technique keeps the content relevant thereby keeping participants interested and engaged.

When you communicate well before and after a session, participants will be more at ease and more likely to share positive feedback about their experience with others. When participants have a good experience with your virtual training, their anecdotal feedback can be used to promote future events. Collect these testimonials and success stories, and share them with all of your stakeholders, especially future participants.

In Summary: Key Points From Chapter 6

- Implementing virtual training is more about changing hearts and minds about online learning than it is about technology.
- Participant preparation is often overlooked, yet it is an essential step to successful virtual training.
- Participants have new responsibilities when learning in the virtual classroom, such as setting up their own workspace and printing their own materials.
- Participants won't pay attention or learn if they are unable to focus during the training class due to their unsuitable learning environment or due to technical challenges. It's important to do everything you can to set them up for success.
- Get the participants' managers involved, and educate them about virtual training.

Checklist 6-1 Sample Participant Preparation

Technical Needs:

- ○ Strong (wired) Internet connection
- ○ Reliable computer or laptop
- ○ Hands-free headset (not a speakerphone)
- ○ Sound card for hearing video playback (if used)
- ○ Software for virtual classroom platform

Other Preparation:

- ○ Find a quiet space to focus and learn.
- ○ Set your devices to "do not disturb" mode (hang sign on door if needed).
- ○ Put away distractions (including "to-do" lists that are in view).
- ○ Close out of email.
- ○ Be sure to test your connection using the provided link at least 72 hours prior to class start time.

Worksheet 6-1 Kickoff Session Sample Agenda

Topic	Content
Welcome	• Brief greeting from facilitator
Introductions	• Interactive exercise, to get to know who's in attendance and begin creating community among participants
Welcome From a Senior Leader	• Share the importance of the training program and its connection to business results • Express commitment to virtual training as a viable learning modality
What to Expect—Content	• Overview of program learning objectives and how the program will be structured (number of sessions, etc.)
What to Expect—Participation	• Set expectations for all about involvement and engagement • Offer tips and suggestions
What to Expect—Platform Tools	• Review of any platform tools not yet used during this session, along with reinforcement of ones already used
Next Steps	• Logistics for next virtual class, along with any assignments to complete between now and then

Remember to invite both the participants and their direct managers.

Keep this session as interactive as possible, both to set expectations and to help participants learn how to use the tools.

Chapter (7)

Create Success Through Logistics

In this chapter, you will learn how to create virtual training success through logistics:

- Recognize the importance of the administrator role.
- Plan logistics according to five key milestones.
- Create a consistent process for virtual training events.
- Consider ongoing maintenance requirements.

Legendary basketball coach John Wooden once said, "It's the little details that are vital. Little things make big things happen" (ESPN, 2010). While he was referring to success in sports, he may have well been talking about virtual training. Paying attention to the details will make the difference between success and failure in your online programs.

When organizations begin to implement virtual training solutions, they often underestimate the amount of logistical details that are required for success. It's a common misperception that virtual training events are easy. Many people think, "What's there to it? Just create a link to the session, send it to participants, and it's ready to go." I have heard similar types of statements from many individuals when they are first getting started in the live online environment.

While it may seem easy from the outside—and that's actually the goal—the amount of time and effort that goes into setting up virtual training should not be taken for granted. Successful virtual training requires thoughtful planning, careful preparation, and diligent execution. Like a figure skater who spins effortlessly or a gymnast who easily flips high in the air, these beautiful and graceful moves only come after hours of preparation. It's the same with virtual training.

In this chapter, we will cover the full scope of required logistics that create success. Some of the items may seem elementary while others should get you thinking on a deeper level. We will also answer the questions: Who does what? And when should they do it?

"It's a lot more administrative work than traditional classroom training because of what it takes to create a positive learning experience."

—Lisa Brodeth Carrick, Executive Director, Comcast University

---

The Coordinator/Administrator Role

In chapter 2, we discussed roles found in typical virtual training rollouts. As a reminder, the coordinator role was defined as: *The administrative person who handles logistical details of virtual training events. This person might administer the organization's LMS (learning management system), as well as communicate with participants before and after an event.*

Many larger training departments employ a "learning coordinator" or administrative assistant to handle these coordination details. While in other organizations, the facilitator or other training professional is responsible for taking care of her own logistics. The training department structure depends upon resources, budgets, headcounts, division of responsibilities, and so on.

Once upon a time, I was a one-person training department for a large global organization. I would have loved to have a learning coordinator to help with all of the details involved with our training programs; however, it wasn't in the budget or even a thought for consideration. On occasion, I was able to tap into administrative help from other departments, but most of the logistics related to training were my responsibility.

Whether the learning coordinator is a separate person in your organization, or someone who wears multiple hats and performs these functions as part of his overall job description, the tasks associated with this administrative role are essential for virtual training success.

The rest of this chapter will explore all of the required logistics in detail. In the meantime, to give you an idea about the types of tasks required, consider this partial list of "hats" an administrative person might wear:

- record keeper

- communication maven

- behind-the-scenes setup coordinator

- knowledge manager

- platform expert

- technical support.

To minimize any confusion between a person who holds a "learning coordi-nator" job title, and others who simply perform administrative responsibilities in addition to their other duties, I will refer to both as the "administrator" from this point forward. In other words, the "administrator role" will mean anyone who is doing logistical tasks, regardless of their actual job title.

Facilitator Role vs. Administrator Role

How do you distinguish between the facilitator's role in a virtual training program and the administrative role, especially if your organization has only one person who does everything—both logistics and facilitation? A quick summary of the differences are:

The facilitator is usually the "face" and "voice" of the virtual training program to the participants. She is the person ultimately responsible for creating the learning experience. The facilitator leads the training event, coaches participants on new skills, delivers the class, and facilitates learning. She directly interacts with participants, typically before, during, and after a training event, particularly if it's a lengthy blended curriculum with multiple sessions.

On the other hand, the administrator usually stays "behind the scenes" of a virtual training program, coordinating resources and ensuring that all class details are cared for. The administrator often does communicate with participants; however, it's with a different purpose than the facilitator communication. It's more of a program manager role. The administrator typically does not get involved with the actual learning process but instead focuses on logistics and other details.

To further illustrate the difference between these roles, consider this scenario: In preparation for next month's virtual training class, the administrator logs into the virtual platform. He creates the event, and generates a link that will be shared with all attendees. As participants register for the class, the administrator ensures that they receive class materials and class connection details.

The facilitator receives the link and registration lists from the administrator, and begins to connect with participants. The facilitator reaches out to introduce herself, welcome them to the training program, and see what questions they have about preparation. The facilitator begins building rapport with the class so that by the time the event starts, there is already a certain comfort level established. The facilitator then delivers the program and guides participants in the learning process.

At the conclusion of the event, the participants receive an email message from the administrator reminding them to complete the online evaluation and offering information about the next course in the series.

Logistics Timeline

Now that we have defined the administrator role, let's consider the specific tasks that should be done by an administrator to make virtual training successful. It's easiest to consider these tasks in terms of when they need to be completed, so I'll review them according to milestones along a virtual class timeline. This logistics timeline can be split into five areas: before the event, just before the event, during the event, at the ending of the event, and after the event.

Before

First, you may be wondering what's meant by "before"—how much before a virtual training session should the administrative preparation begin? I hesitate to give an exact timeframe because it depends upon a number of factors, such as the complexity of the virtual training initiative and whether or not this is your first virtual training rollout. However, "before" is probably much earlier than you think.

For example, if you have a virtual training class that's part of a six-week blended learning curriculum, and it requires prereading assignments prior to each virtual session, then the administrative details will be more than if you have just a one-time virtual session. Also, if it's a brand new virtual training program, and you are delivering it for the first time, then there will be more logistics to work out than if you have an existing established program.

For any type of virtual training program—lengthy curriculums or one-time events—here are the main pre-event logistics to consider and prepare for during the "before" phase:

- initial team meeting

- marketing/advertising

- registration

- material distribution

- virtual classroom setup

- communication with participants

- practice/rehearsal.

Let's look in more detail at each one.

"Some people think that once the technology is set, you're done. But there's just so much that happens behind the scenes to make virtual training look easy."

—Peggy Page, Design Group Manager, TD Bank

Initial Team Meeting

Just like a typical project begins with a project setup meeting, a first-time virtual training rollout should begin with an initial meeting that includes all individuals who will be involved with its logistics. This list may include facilitators, producers, administrators, designers, IT, and all other program stakeholders. The purpose of this meeting is to establish roles, responsibilities, expectations, and communication methods. Once your organization gets into an operating rhythm for virtual training logistics, this initial meeting will no longer be needed. For new programs, it's highly recommended.

The initial meeting agenda should focus on a walk-through of the administrative tasks and their timeline for completion. It should also focus on the specifics of who exactly will do what and when. Meeting participants should agree upon role clarification and strategies for dealing with any plan deviations that may arise.

Marketing/Advertising

Another key task that may be needed for your virtual training is a targeted marketing and advertising campaign. The point of this campaign is to increase awareness of the training program and its benefits to participants and other interested stakeholders. It's to motivate participants to get involved early on and actively engage in the learning process. And it can also be used to communicate relevant details of interest, such as date and time commitments.

If your participants are obligated to attend the virtual training due to a job requirement, then the marketing will not be quite as important than if participants can choose to attend based on open enrollment. An open enrollment program marketing campaign will need to emphasize direct benefits to the potential participants based on expected learning outcomes. The marketing campaign will also be different if participants are nominated by their manager to attend, such as for a high-potential leadership program. In that case, the main advertising would be directed to managers, with emphasis on why they should send their employees to this training program.

The actual tasks associated with marketing a training program include:

- Writing the program advertising text and graphics: What will you say about the program?

- Choosing marketing methods: social media, website listing, paper flyers in visible locations, or others.

- Posting the marketing content to chosen locations.

While these marketing tasks are the same for traditional and virtual training programs, a critical point not to be missed is that you are marketing a **virtual** training program. If virtual training is a new way of learning for your organization, then it will be essential for your marketing to focus on the benefits new modality. Your marketing campaign will be for both awareness of the training program and education on the new modality.

One of my clients was implementing a communication skills blended training curriculum, and as part of its design I created a one-page marketing document that they could use to advertise the program. The document clearly articulated the program outcomes and reasons to attend. It also described the unique virtual approach and the benefits of learning online. My client successfully used this document to communicate the program to their target audience.

Registration

Once the program advertising has begun, the administrator needs to keep track of registrations and enrollments. If the training program has any prerequisite requirements, then they will also need to ensure each registrant meets the qualifications. In its simplest form, registrations can be tracked in a spreadsheet. Participants could contact the administrator by phone call, text, or email to sign up for the program. The spreadsheet would track enrollment data along with participant details. It could then also be used to track attendance after the program.

If your organization uses a learning management system (LMS), then the registration process can be automated. Participants could sign up online and their registration information would be captured. In this case, the LMS would need to be prepared. Everything needs to be loaded into the LMS: course description, program information, materials, and all other communication documents that participants should see upon registration.

"Your LMS can be a huge time-saver for managing registrations and communications for virtual events, especially if it integrates directly with your virtual classroom platform. Most LMS's can automate and track registrations and:

- *send registration confirmation and reminder emails*

- *distribute materials before and after an event*

- *record attendance from the virtual event*

- *distribute and track results of evaluations and assessments."*

—Wendy Gates Corbett, Global Training Director

Material Distribution

Material distribution also belongs to the list of key logistical tasks that need to be considered before a virtual training event. This category includes all participant materials that need to be distributed or printed before the class.

You may remember that chapter 4 includes a lengthy discussion of the benefits of providing reference materials to participants. It also discusses the choice between asking participants to print them ahead of time or shipping preprinted materials directly to them. Either way, there is administrative work to be done for material distribution. If you ask participants to print their own class materials, then those materials need to either be sent via email or they need to be loaded into a central repository (a document sharing site or a LMS) that's accessible to everyone. Participants need explicit instructions on how to access the files and any special printing instructions. The more advance notice you give to participants, the better, so that they have time to complete this task. And of course, if you are planning to ship books or other printed files to participants, then all of those logistics need to be done.

According to Darlene Christopher, Knowledge & Learning Officer at the WorldBank, it's important to plan out material distribution well in advance, especially with global participants. For some classes, Darlene's administrator will send each participant a pen and custom notepad along with the class materials. The administrator also sends an email message, to confirm material receipt. While only a few of their virtual classes include this physical mailing, the administrative work for it needs to be planned in advance.

LMS Administration

If your organization has a learning management system (LMS) then many of these pre-event logistics can be automated. If the LMS administrator is part of the training department, or even the same person as the learning coordinator, then you may be able to streamline some of the responsibilities associated with virtual training logistical tasks. This is a big advantage to using a LMS.

However, there are pros and cons to using a LMS for complete automation of virtual training logistics. The pros seem obvious— automation, economies of scale, and time saved. Yet the drawbacks of an automated system include less personalized content and potential challenges for some learners who may not have easy access to the Internet. Also, depending upon its features, the LMS may or may not be customizable for virtual or blended learning solutions.

Regardless, if your organization uses a LMS, consider which virtual training logistics can be automated in order to save administrative time.

Virtual Classroom Setup

The next administrative step is setting up the virtual classroom, which can be broken down into two parts:

- creating the training event using the virtual classroom platform's administrative tools

- loading training content into the virtual classroom.

The person performing this logistical task needs to be very well versed in the virtual platform's administrative features so that they can accurately set up the event.

Creating the Event

Each individual event that will occur needs to be initiated in the virtual classroom platform. This step initiates a link that can be shared with participants. The exact steps to complete this task depend upon your platform; however, most are similar in form and function. A person with administrative rights to the virtual platform logs into the program and creates a new event. They enter the date, time, and estimated length of the session. They confirm audio details, and may be able to preset participant privileges. They can also set access rights for facilitators, producers, and other participants. Once the online event has been created, the connection link can be shared with everyone who needs it.

Figure 7-1 Adobe Connect Administrative Setup

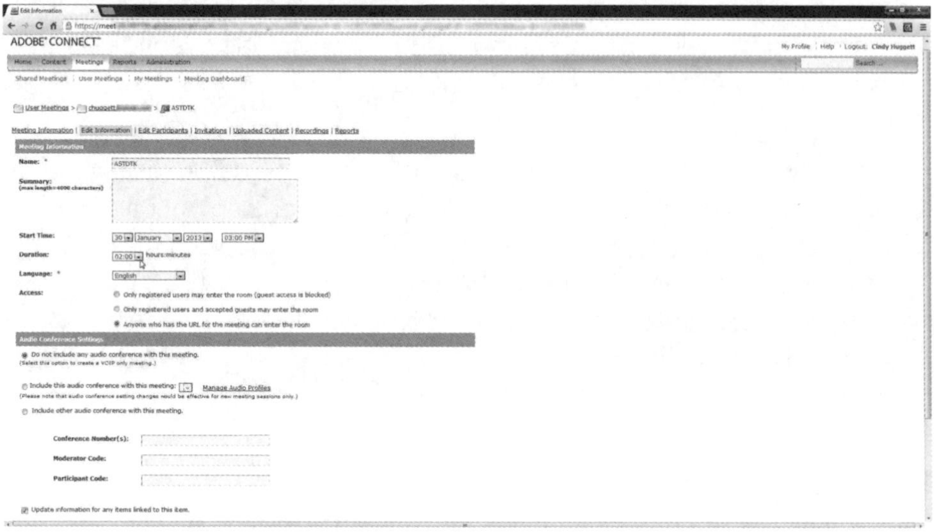

Loading Training Content

Next, the actual training content needs to be loaded into the virtual classroom. Some platforms allow this step to be done days or weeks in advance of the session. Other platforms only allow it to be done right before the session begins. If there are multiple people in your organization performing administrative tasks, this is one sub-step that many facilitators take responsibility for, instead of the learning coordinator. The person who completes this task needs to have access to facilitator materials, including slides, poll questions, and any other documents that will be needed.

When facilitating a virtual class, I prefer to load my own training content into the classroom as part of my pre-event setup. It would save me time if someone else took on that responsibility. Yet there's something about the routine of setting up my own classroom that is appealing to me. So even if I have administrative assistance, this is one task that I enjoy doing myself before class begins.

The facilitator guide should include all setup information for the class and instructions for loading content online. If an administrator loads training content into the classroom, then they will need to have access to the materials and should follow the facilitator guide instructions.

Virtual Classrooms: One-Time Use vs. Perpetual

In some platforms, the event "room" can only be used one time, at the specific date and time selected during the initial setup. However, if the event room can be used over and over again for multiple events, then it's considered a perpetual classroom.

The advantage to a perpetual classroom is that it only needs to be set up one time. After the classroom is used for an event, it only needs to be cleaned (that is, clearing answers to poll questions, erasing annotations, and so on) before the next use. Another advantage of perpetual classrooms is that the same link could be used for a series of events. So if you have a blended curriculum with multiple events, only one link has to be shared with everyone.

Communicating With Participants

This administrative task—communicating connection details and other session logistics—is most often done via email. Most virtual classroom platforms generate an email message when a session link is created; but this standardized message often has very little information besides connection details. It's typically not enough to inspire your participants to get involved. Therefore, take the opportunity to create your own set of messages to communicate session logistics.

As we discussed in chapter 4, an interactive virtual class should be engaging from the moment that your participants register for it. You can use all of your session logistics communications to set and reinforce expectations that it's going to be an active learning experience. Of course, be sure to include links and connection details as well. For example, the first message a participant receives upon class enrollment could start creating interactivity by inviting them to do one or more of the following:

- Engage with other participants on a discussion board.

- Print a handout with a relevant pre-class exercise, which will be referred to during class.

- Respond to a topic-related question or two, and bring the answers with them to class.

- Send questions they have about the topic to the facilitator.

When sending this first communication message, keep in mind the participants and their likelihood of actually reading it and completing any included assignments. They will be more apt to open the message if the subject line is interesting. In his book, *To Sell Is Human,* author Dan Pink observes that the subject line of an email message is an important factor in whether or not a message will be opened. Based on proven research from Carnegie Mellon, Dan recommends that subject lines either be perceived as useful or instill curiosity. And based on research from Brian Clark, he also recommends that subject lines should be specific (Pink, 2012, 166-167). So take time to carefully craft subject lines that are most likely to be opened by participants. For example, the email subject line of your reminder message for a time management virtual class might read "Today's class will teach you how to gain an extra hour of time every day."

After initial class connection details have been shared, the administrator should also send periodic reminder messages. These reminders should not only include class logistical information and preparation assignments, but also continued reinforcement that the session will be interactive.

For example, you could word the message to remind participants that they should prepare to be hands-on during the session and that you'll expect them to respond often. Remind them to close out of their email and other programs at the start of the session so they can give the class their full attention. Consider sending them a "Do not disturb—training in session" sign that they could hang on their office door. By communicating these expectations prior to the session, participants will not be blindsided when they are asked to jump in 'with both feet' when the virtual training class begins.

The number of reminders sent depends upon how far in advance participants have registered. You want to find a balance between overloading an email inbox and keeping the training top of mind. At least one reminder should be sent a few business days prior to the session.

Tips for Communicating With Participants

Consider both *what* you communicate (content), and *how* you communicate it (style).

Content

Make all of your communication easy to read with clear and concise text. Take a lesson from marketing professionals who use appealing words and catch phrases to gain attention.

You can do some very simple things to make data easy to read in an email message. For example, if there are strings of numbers that have to be used, such as an event or conference call passcode, then separate numbers into chunks (i.e. "123 45 6789" instead of "123456789"). It's easier on the eyes.

Also, consider carefully if you will include the session's phone number and passcode along with the web link. In most cases, it isn't necessary because the audio information will be displayed on screen once a participant joins the virtual classroom. In fact, some platform audio features may not be available if the participants dial in separately, so it's extra important that they log into the session first and then follow the audio prompts. By not listing the phone connection you can force participants to join the web first.

In addition, include class materials, event links, and technical support information in every communication you have with participants. That way, if they have to search for this information, they will easily find it.

Style

Listen to virtual training experts Treion Muller and Matt Murdoch, who say it best by encouraging us to "shut down the ugly" when communicating with participants about virtual training events. Their fantastic book, *The Webinar Manifesto* (2013), urges us to "write beautiful words" and "design beautiful graphics" for every communication piece we send. When administrators follow this advice, it will increase the likelihood of their messages being read.

Practice/Rehearsal

Prior to the first virtual training event, there should be at least one practice or rehearsal. This allows everyone involved a chance to test connectivity and run through the content in a "dress rehearsal" fashion. It also gives opportunity for the facilitator and producer to talk through how they will partner together.

While mostly important for facilitator and producer to attend the pre-event rehearsals, an administrator sometimes attends these sessions as an observer. And of course, if the administrator is wearing the producer and/or the facilitator hat, then it's a given that she will be in attendance.

The most important role of the administrator for practice and rehearsals is to ensure that the virtual classroom links are created, the content is loaded, and the classroom is ready for the practice. Add this task as one more item to the list of things that need to be done before a virtual training event.

Just Before

Moving to the timeframe of "just before," this section captures all of the logistics that should be done on the day of the event. In some ways, it's like the production of a show that has a countdown clock, with many last minute details to handle.

First, it's always a good idea to send a day-of-event reminder message to participants. In fact, the administrator may even want to send a reminder message to the facilitators and anyone else who has a supporting role in the training. This last minute check-in helps everyone have the connection details at their fingertips.

Second, if the virtual classroom platform does not allow for content loading prior to the event, then this task needs to be completed just before the class. I recommend the host log in and set up approximately 60 minutes prior to the session start time. While 60 minutes may seem extreme, its only 15 minutes more than my normal recommended host log-in time of 45 minutes prior to a session. If it still seems extreme, compare it to a traditional face-to-face class, where the facilitator almost always shows up an hour prior to start time to complete setup and other logistical tasks before the participants arrive. It's the same principle in the virtual classroom. Err on the side of caution, especially if the classroom needs to have content loaded, participant features enabled, and polls or other activities created.

What's a "Host"?

Virtual classroom platforms assign a role to every person who joins an online session. Each role has different privilege levels for using the platform tools. Specific role names vary from program to program, for example one program might use the name "host" while another uses the name "presenter." Regardless of the actual name, the "host" role has the most control over the class. She can start and end sessions, determine who has presenter rights, and grant extra privileges (such as annotation rights) to attendees.

The administrative person who logs in early must have "host" privileges to the platform so that they can start (sometimes called "open") the classroom. He should then double-check all of the content and audio connections. Most of the time everything will be there as expected, but it's a good idea to double check.

Once the session is open, the next step is preparing to greet participants. Hopefully you have encouraged participants to join at least 10 minutes early. As we established in chapter 4 on design, even before the official start time, the class has already begun. The goal is immediate engagement once participants connect to the session.

It's the facilitator who should welcome participants to class, while the producer assists with any connection or technical challenges. The administrative tasks associated with this time period include sending any last minute links, connection details, or materials to participants who may need them. Even if the administrator is not planning to be online, sometimes she will need to pitch in and help out with the session if technical issues arise. She should keep a schedule of classes and be available or on-call, especially if the facilitator is solo without a producer. Think of it like a partnership, and when it's time to serve the customers (in other words, the participants), then "all hands on deck" may be needed.

For example, recently I was just about to begin a virtual training class when the audio connection stopped working. On top of that, several participants mistakenly had an incorrect link to join the session. My producer and I needed an extra set of hands to communicate with participants, and so we called upon the administrator to jump in and assist. We were able to quickly resolve the situation and class started only a few minutes late. This type of partnership requires flexibility on everyone's part, to ensure a fantastic learning experience for participants. By working together as a team the participants will have a more seamless experience. If you do not have a separate administrator to help with these last minute details, use this idea from Citrix GoToTraining's Kelley Eason: Set your email out-of-office message to include the connection details of the virtual training session so that anyone who contacts you for this information will automatically receive it.

During

By the time the session begins, much of the logistics work is done. But there are a few key administrative tasks that may need to be completed during a session.

First, most classes require capturing participant attendance for record keeping. The administrator can join the session briefly to note which participants have signed in. Alternatively, the facilitator could ask each participant to type their name in chat (via an introduction-type activity), and then take a screen shot or email the chat window contents to the administrator.

If other unexpected technical challenges arise during a session, the administrator might need to stay "on call" to assist. For example, he may need to call upon a local IT contact in the same building as a remote participant who can offer immediate technical assistance. Or he may need to find international dialing instructions for a participant who needs them. And in an emergency, the administrator may need to find another facilitator at the last minute to fill in. While these situations might be extreme, having the administrator available during a session could make the difference between success and frustration. Obviously in a large organization there may be multiple sessions going on at once that an administrator may need to handle. In this case, keeping an accurate calendar of events is essential.

Ending

Near the end of a virtual training session, there are four short but important administrative tasks to consider:

- Distribute reference materials.
- Conduct knowledge assessments.
- Provide class evaluations.
- Share "what's next" (for blended curriculums).

These tasks can be done in any order, whichever makes the most sense for the program design.

Distribute Reference Materials

Use the virtual classroom platform's file sharing tools to give participants access to reference materials, additional handouts, or job aids associated with the class. If a file sharing feature is not available, or if it cannot be set up ahead of time, then have the administrator manually send these documents to participants at the end of class. If you have multiple people completing administrative tasks, ensure they all know about your position on what specific materials should be shared with participants. As advocated in chapter 4, the slides are part of the facilitator guide and typically not shared with participants. If you have the urge to share slides, then consider whether or not you have a presentation instead of a training class.

Conduct Knowledge Assessments

Another end-of-class detail is the completion of assessments or knowledge exams. While the facilitator often takes ownership of this task, it's listed here with logistics to be sure it's handled. Many virtual classroom platforms have built-in tools for these assessments, usually part of the polling or "quiz" feature. The actual content for the assessment comes from the class design and should be detailed in the facilitator guide. The administrative task is to execute the assessment and capture participant scores.

If the virtual classroom platform does not have a quiz feature, then this step may be accomplished through a third-party assessment tool. In that case, a link to the exam would need to be distributed to participants. In some cases it's possible for a LMS to communicate with the quiz feature (internal or external) and automatically record results. If not, then the administrator may need to manually capture this information.

Provide Class Evaluations

The next end-of-class administrative detail is the class evaluation to gather participant feedback. If you are also using knowledge assessments, then you might choose to combine the end-of-class evaluation together into one form. The virtual classroom tools or a third-party tool should be used to get this feedback. A best practice is to allow time at the end of a session, before the scheduled stop time, for participants to complete these forms. That means if the class is scheduled for 60 minutes, the evaluation would begin at least by the 55-minute mark. And if the knowledge assessment is combined together with the evaluation, then even more time may be needed. Hopefully the course design allows for the right amount of time.

"We end class at least three to five minutes early so that participants have time to complete the evaluation form. This means we have nearly a 100 percent completion rate."

—**Justin Patton, Master Facilitator, YUM! University**

Share What's Next

Finally, if the event has a post-class assignment or is part of a blended curriculum, participants need to know the next step in the process. They may already be aware, but it's always a good idea to have a reminder. By communicating "what's next" at the end of the session, participants will be more likely to remember and take action. This administrative task can be completed through a number of methods:

- Post a slide in the classroom with "next step" details on it.
- Share a document with relevant details.
- Send an email reminder message to their inbox.
- Provide a graphic showing the next step.
- Send a calendar reminder for a time-based next event.

After

Once a virtual session has completed, there are three main administrative tasks to complete. First, if there are any tasks from the "ending" section that did not get done before the end of class, do those now. This includes sharing reference materials, assignments, assessments, evaluations, and next step items.

Next, the classroom should be closed down properly. If any items need to be saved, such as participant annotations on the whiteboard, chat window responses, or answers to poll questions, do that before ending the session. If you are using a perpetual virtual classroom, clean it up to make it ready for its next use. Items that should be refreshed include:

- clear answers to poll questions
- erase whiteboards
- rewind video/media files
- clear slide annotations
- refresh breakout rooms.

Finally, the administrator should lead a "lessons learned" meeting at some point after the session. It gives an opportunity for the virtual training team to distill evaluation feedback, provide insight to facilitators, and give course review information to designers. The administrator would take notes on items that could be improved, changed, or updated, along with any other suggestions for improvement to the content or process for the next time.

Idea: Turning Synchronous Classes into Perpetual Asynchronous Sessions

According to Ken Hubbell, Senior Manager of Learning Technology at Ingersoll Rand, some of their virtual training classes are recorded and preserved as asynchronous lessons. Since watching a playback of a live online class is not the best way to learn, they repurpose the synchronous sessions in a way that makes sense for offline viewing.

Ideally, they run a virtual class at least three times, recording each one. Afterward, an administrator watches the recordings, notes the highlights, and captures common questions asked. They then take the highlight segments or modules of each class and weave them together to create a shorter recording or series of modules that can be posted and viewed or incorporated into other courses.

Creating an Ongoing Administrative Process

Assuming that your organization will hold more than one virtual training event, then creating a standard process for all of these administrative tasks will be a useful endeavor. The process should delineate what do to, who will do it, and when it will happen along the logistics timeline. A consistent process will guide the administrator along as he or she performs each task.

It's key to keep your process simple! Too much complexity will only create confusion and bog down the entire process. An organization I worked with recently had good intentions when creating their virtual training administrative process. However, over time it became so complex and confusing that no one was able to follow it.

Their process began when they created a short checklist for who would be responsible for creating the virtual event link and sending it out to participants. They allowed for exceptions to the process depending upon the event because some facilitators also took on administrative responsibilities. Then, they expanded their virtual training offerings to include blended curriculums and multi-event sessions, for which they created a different process. In other words, one administrative process applied to single-session virtual events, while a separate process applied when it was a multiple-session virtual event. They continued to allow exceptions to both processes based upon numerous factors that seemed to make sense at the time. Unfortunately, what happened is that no one actually knew which process to follow, and when it would or would not be used. They eventually realized this problem and streamlined everything into one simple process. The moral of this story is to keep your processes simple so that they will be followed.

In addition, create a process that allows for a rhythm that is easily replicated. If it's your organization's first virtual training rollout, keep notes on what works and what doesn't work. Gather feedback from your participants, and all other stakeholders, to help you make those decisions. Then use the "lessons learned" meeting so that you can reflect on the tasks, timeline, and other details that had impact on your program.

If multiple people will be involved in your typical virtual training rollout, consider using a simple RACI model to help you determine who has Responsibility, who needs to give Authorization, who needs to Contribute, and who just needs to be kept Informed. RACI models are commonly used in project management plans to easily identify roles and responsibilities. When used and followed, they can add tremendous value.

Task	Responsibility	Authorization	Contribute	Informed
Table 7-1 Sample RACI Chart for Virtual Training Logistics				
Create event links				
Send pre-event communications				
Load content into the virtual classroom				

If you already have a process in place for your virtual training, step back and take a look at it. Use "start, stop, continue" as a method to evaluate your process. In other words, make a list of logistical things you need to *start* doing, things you should *stop* doing (because they are redundant or not needed), and things you should *continue* doing. This simple method can revitalize and streamline your current processes so that they are as useful as possible.

Ongoing Maintenance

Another category of administrative tasks associated with virtual training are not tied to specific training events, but instead are more general details that must be managed. These items include:

- vendor contracts
- technology updates
- document controls.

It's important to designate someone in the organization to be responsible for each of these items.

Vendor Contracts

Most virtual training platforms are purchased on a subscription basis, under contract terms that dictate the length of time for service. Periodically these contracts should be reviewed to ensure service terms are met. Also, when it's time for the contract to be renewed, someone needs to negotiate with the vendor and update the terms. This task might be relegated to your organization's purchasing group or IT department.

Yet someone in the training function should stay involved with any discussions or negotiations, just like they were during the initial decision-making process.

Technology Updates

When a virtual classroom platform updates its software to a new version, someone needs to track what features have changed and communicate that to everyone in the organization who uses it. Whether the changes are minor or major, facilitators and designers need to know so that they can adjust and adapt as needed. For example, a platform software upgrade may require users to download a new add-on upon the next launch. Or, there may be a revision to how tools or features are used. Even a small change, such as how a participant uses the eraser tool on a whiteboard or how a facilitator can display a poll question, could have ripple effects on how a class activity works. Therefore, it's important to track software version changes and communicate them immediately.

Document Controls

Finally, as class materials are updated by designers, there must be version control of all associated class materials. Many organizations will establish a set period of time for when changes can be made to course materials. However, since most virtual classes use electronic documents, it's easy to make fast updates based on participant feedback. Someone needs to track these changes and distribute the revised materials. Ideally, an administrative person is kept informed so that this task can be completed.

One Organization's Story

According to Trish Carr, LMS Administrator at YUM! University, their virtual training programs run smoothly because of the work done by their behind-the-scenes team. Trish's goal is to "set up the session for success."

When a virtual training session needs to be scheduled, a facilitator completes an online form to request assistance from Trish's team. Using the form data, someone from the team will set up the virtual classroom and all associated data in the learning management system. The facilitator then receives the link and participants are able to register for the class.

Trish will then schedule someone from her team to join the class for at least the first 10 to 15 minutes to ensure everyone is able to log in and connect to the session. They help the facilitator and participants with any technical issues that may arise.

Even though the participants rarely communicate directly with the behind-the-scenes team, the detailed work they do directly impacts a participant's learning experience. It's an important team role that contributes to success.

In Summary: Key Points From Chapter 7

- It's common to underestimate the amount of logistical details that are required for virtual training success.
- The administrator role performs tasks such as record keeping, communication, setup coordination, and platform support. Even if multiple people perform the administrator role, these logistics need to be done.
- Begin planning for logistics as far in advance as possible.
- A learning management system (LMS) can automate many logistical tasks; however, a personalized human touch creates value.
- Carefully craft participant communication pieces.
- Keep your administrative processes simple.

Checklist 7-1 Virtual Training Logistics

Before

- ○ Initial team meeting to plan logistics
    - ○ Date and time: _____
    - ○ Invitation List: _____
- ○ Marketing/advertising
    - ○ Where? _____
    - ○ How? _____
    - ○ When? _____
- ○ Registration
- ○ Material distribution
- ○ Virtual classroom setup
- ○ Participant communication
    - ○ #1: _____
    - ○ #2: _____
    - ○ #3: _____
- ○ Practice/rehearsal
    - ○ Date and time: _____
    - ○ Invitation list: _____

Just Before

- ○ Day of event: reminder message
- ○ Load content into virtual classroom (if not done in "Before" stage)
- ○ Log in 45-60 minutes prior to start time
- ○ Greet and begin to engage participants
- ○ Start class

During

- ○ Capture participant attendance
- ○ Be prepared to assist as needed with technical challenges

Ending

- ○ Distribute reference materials
- ○ Conduct knowledge assessments
- ○ Provide class evaluations
- ○ Share what's next

After

- ○ Close and clean up virtual classroom
- ○ Record keeping
- ○ Hold "lessons learned" meeting to improve for next time

Chapter (8)

Special Considerations: Global Issues, Evaluation Metrics, and Future Trends

---

In this chapter, you will learn special considerations for virtual training:

- Consider the unique concerns for global virtual training rollouts.
- Evaluate the success of virtual training.
- Look ahead at three key trends to watch for the future of virtual training.

When beginning a journey to a new destination, most people plan ahead of time to make the trip a success. They preview a map or set their navigation system to determine the best route to get there. They estimate the amount of time it will take for the trip, and plan accordingly. When traffic roadblocks or other obstacles arise, they use the tools at their disposal to expertly navigate around them. And for some, the fun part of the journey is to find the unexpected along the way, and they enjoy the process as much as the final destination.

The same things can occur during a virtual training rollout. When you take the time to properly prepare for virtual training, you create a road map to success. When roadblocks or obstacles arise, you use resources to help you navigate around them. And for many training professionals, they enjoy the entire virtual training process.

This chapter addresses three specific considerations to factor into your virtual training journey. Whether you have an easy road or an uphill climb, review each of these three items and apply what is useful to your situation. Use these tips to ensure you will find the final destination—and the process to get there—meets and exceeds expectations.

Global Considerations

One of the biggest benefits of virtual training is its ability to reach across borders and draw geographically dispersed people together. Training topics can be offered to those who wouldn't otherwise be able to attend a class. Diverse cultures can meet together to discuss common issues. Communication between siloed individuals or groups can improve as a result of spending time together learning new things.

Yet these benefits also come with their own unique set of challenges. When you have an audience that speaks different languages, new training topics can present language challenges. Diverse cultures can have differing expectations about training. And individuals may not be able to connect well due to technology or other communication barriers. While the challenges of delivering virtual training to global audiences may seem daunting and enough to discourage an organization from trying it, the benefits far outweigh the drawbacks. So let's look at several strategies and tips for successfully designing, delivering, and implementing virtual training to a global audience.

Types of Global Virtual Training

There are several ways you might think about "global" virtual training. First, it could be a U.S. organization or a U.S.-based trainer who delivers training to a targeted global audience. In other words, the organization and trainer may be based in San Jose, California while the participants are in Brazil, Poland, or some other country.

In this scenario, it would be important to "localize" the training for the target audience. The design would be modified to fit the audience expectations. It's very similar to what an organization would do if a trainer traveled to that location to deliver an in-person session. For example, I recently delivered a virtual training session to a European audience, and changed several words on my slides from American English to British English (recognize became recognise and color became colour).

Second, "global" virtual training could also refer to any organization or trainer in any location delivering training to international audience. Participants could join the session from the U.S., Asia, Europe, Africa, or anywhere. The distinction for this group is that the audience includes a mix of cultures and native languages.

In this scenario, it would be important to diversify your approach to appeal to wide audiences. The tips and techniques in this chapter will help you consider options for this second type of global training.

Design Issues for Global Training

All of the design principles learned in chapter 4 apply regardless of your participants' geographic location. Good virtual training design creates a highly interactive participant experience that is focused on learning outcomes. However, to appeal to a culturally diverse audience, factor in these five additional design techniques:

- Recognize different perceptions about virtual training.

- Allow for extra communication time during a session.

- Use culturally neutral examples and graphics.

- Choose scenario character names recognizable to a diverse audience.

- Send materials ahead of time to minimize potential language barriers.

Recognize Different Perceptions About Virtual Training

Around the world, different cultures have different views of training. These views naturally transfer to perceptions of virtual training. For example, many Americans tend to have an informal style and consider the facilitator a peer or colleague, which influences how they interact. They might be more willing to engage in dialogue, interrupt to make a statement, and ask questions more freely. In contrast, some other cultures view the facilitator as the expert and would not interrupt even if they had an important comment to share. They may hesitate to ask questions, or wait for an invitation to participate during a virtual session. (Of course, this specific generalization of Americans as compared to other cultures is not meant to stereotype, since there are naturally exceptions to this rule in all cultures. My goal is only to make the point that diversity of thought and experience increases when a global audience is involved.)

When Global Training Director Wendy Gates Corbett needed to facilitate a virtual session to a global audience, she factored these potential cultural differences into her scheduling decisions. She knew she needed three different sessions in order to accommodate multiple time zones. So she scheduled the North America session first, the Europe/Middle East session second, and finally the Asia/Pacific session.

169

Since her Asia/Pacific audience was often the quietest group, she would be able to include common questions and examples from the earlier sessions as needed.

So what's a designer to do when designing a virtual training program that will be used for a global audience? Make it easy and comfortable for participants to speak up during class by establishing ground rules and setting expectations. Ask for reactions to scenarios and examples. Design activities that invite conversation in safe ways, such as using paired chat exercises and small group breakout rooms. Emphasize use of the chat feature for both public and private communication. Make liberal use of the status indicator features (raise hand, agree/disagree, and others) for participants to voice opinions without actually using their voice. These techniques are good for every audience, but especially important for culturally diverse ones.

Darlene Christopher, Global Knowledge Officer at the World Bank, recommends that with global audiences we "ask participants to reflect on a concept" before introducing it (2012). This reflection time can be accomplished through a poll, a graphic, or an interesting question. Darlene's technique both gives participants the opportunity to think about the content and respond in a thoughtful way. It helps keeps them engaged in the class.

Allow for Extra Communication Time During a Session

When a session is delivered in English to participants who speak English as a second language, or when multiple languages are represented during a session, extra communication time will be needed. The participants may need a few extra seconds to translate or mentally process an unfamiliar word, or to compose their chat response to a question. They also might need more time to read a poll question and all of the choices before submitting their answer. All of these extra few seconds add up to longer activity times and therefore longer class times.

David Smith, Global Director for Virtual Learning Solutions, TMA World, shares that *"with a multicultural audience, things will take longer. With a U.S. audience, you might be able to give two minutes for a reading activity, but a mixed audience probably needs closer to three minutes."*

The design challenge with a mixed language audience is to not slow down the class too much, which could lead a loss of interest from those who do speak the language. If the timing moves too slowly to maintain their interactivity, they may lose interest and disengage from the session. The key is finding a balance between too fast and too slow.

"When designing training for a global audience, I may still plan for a one-hour session but keep the content time shorter to allow for extra conversation and comprehension time."

—**Wendy Gates Corbett, Global Training Director**

Use Culturally Neutral Examples and Graphics

When designing virtual training for global participants, pay attention to any cultural references that may deliberately (or even inadvertently) be included. An American football analogy may work fine for a U.S. audience, but global participants may not fully understand it. Designing an activity based on a popular U.S. game show could be fun, unless the rules are confusing to those not as familiar with it. Similarly, avoid pop culture references that won't be recognized by a global audience. Television shows, games, cartoons, and the like are all potential avenues for misunderstanding.

Even something as small as word choice can make a difference in comprehension and acceptance. For example, there is an activity I like to design into in my virtual train-the-trainer classes that illustrates how we give and receive instructions. I ask participants to take pen and paper, imagine they are at the office, and they need to write down "directions to their home" for someone who needs to get there. (We then debrief how they wrote down the instructions—did they draw a visual map, list out step-by-step turns, or something else altogether?) The point in this example is the deliberate word choice of "to your home" instead of "to your house." Home is a more generic, relatable term than house. And in a global setting, the word choice would make more sense to participants.

Also take care with graphics, such as photos or clip art that may be included on a slide. Select graphics that will not cause offense or be controversial. For instance, it's best to avoid choosing photos of hand gestures to ensure that you have not accidentally selected something inappropriate. I learned this lesson the hard way a few years ago when I spoke to a virtual global audience, and used the phrase "rule of thumb" along with a "thumbs up" graphic on my slide. Several participants let me know that both the phrase and the graphic were could be perceived as offensive in their culture, and I immediately apologized before moving on.

"I have found truth in the phrase 'a picture is worth a thousand words'—especially when it comes to global audiences, and, when it comes to subject matter experts trying to describe a new procedure or a change in process to that audience."

—Jeff Robinson, Global Talent Management, Covance Laboratories, Inc.

Choose Scenario Character Names Recognizable to a Diverse Audience

Similar to using culturally neutral examples and graphics, when writing role plays or case studies for virtual classes, a designer should take care to select names for characters that will be recognized by a diverse audience. If it's an interpersonal skills course that will have a manager-employee dialogue to use during practice, choose everyday names for the characters. Also be sure to select a variety of names that represent multiple cultures. So instead of naming your characters traditional American names like "Peter" or "Mike," you might select other names such as "Pritha" or "Akido."

One of my favorite sources for finding names is the popular baby names list found on *Wikipedia*. I especially like to select names that are popular in more than one language such as "Adam" or "Maria." Being intentional about your name choices will help localize the content and help participants relate more easily to the scenario.

Send Materials Ahead of Time to Minimize Potential Language Barriers

If your content contains many technical or unfamiliar words, consider sending the participant handouts well in advance of the session. Let participants know that the session will be conducted in English (or whichever language will be used). Include instructions for an extra pre-session assignment to review the handout so that participants can look up those words and translate them into their native language.

Likewise, when designing materials for global audiences, avoid jargon and spell out all acronyms. Leave enough white space on each handout page so that participants have room to take additional translation notes.

Using Translators?

One of my clients recently asked about the possibility of inviting an interpreter to translate one of her virtual training classes, so that participants who do not speak English could participate. My recommendation was, "No, it's not a best practice." Here's why:

Imagine a typical virtual training class of 15 participants who all need to learn a new skill. Let's say most of the group speaks English, while a handful speak only Spanish. Handout materials could be distributed in both English and Spanish to accommodate both languages. However, during the live delivery, a facilitator would need to pause every few minutes for the translator to catch up. A translator would need to explain not only the facilitator's words but also the on-screen activities (such as poll questions or exercise instructions). This time lag could be disengaging to both groups, which in turn would interfere with the goal of a highly interactive session. The potential for participants to "check out" while their native language is not spoken could be detrimental to meeting the session goals.

While translators may be an option for one-way presentations or webcasts, they are not the best solution for interactive virtual training. A better solution would be to hold two separate virtual training sessions—one in English and one in Spanish—and invite the appropriate audience to each. Another potential solution would be to use a producer who speaks multiple languages, who could periodically help participants with an unfamiliar word during a session.

Delivery Issues for Global Training

All of the delivery principles learned in chapter 5 apply regardless of your participants' geographic location. Effective virtual facilitators create a comfortable environment while engaging participants in their own learning. However, to appeal to a culturally diverse audience, factor in these three additional delivery techniques:

- Create a comfortable learning environment.

- Use clear language.

- Recognize cultural differences.

Create a Comfortable Learning Environment

Since a multicultural audience might have differing expectations about their participation in training, virtual facilitators need to take extra care to build rapport and establish participation ground rules at the start of a session. They should strive to make everyone feel comfortable engaging with each other despite any language barriers that may get in the way of learning.

One easy technique is to invite participants to respond either verbally or in the chat window, whichever is their preference. This opens up the door to more comfortable communication. For example, the facilitator might ask a question and then specifically say, "You can either respond in the chat window or by speaking verbally." This simple invitation allows participants to choose their response method and keep the classroom comfortable.

Virtual facilitators should also inform learners about any participation expectations, such as "expect to be called upon during class." Remember that while calling on someone by name can help maintain interest and engagement in the session, it's also extremely important to maintain a comfortable learning environment. Therefore, ensure that any direct questions asked have no right or wrong answer. Their point should be to increase participation, not to put someone on the spot.

In addition, virtual facilitators should be open-minded about how individuals from another culture might approach a situation. It may not be the way you would handle it, yet it may be right on target for their unique scenario. For example, I recently delivered a virtual class on performance management to a mostly Korean audience. When we discussed how to assign performance ratings, several participants were more concerned about their team's collective performance than individual employee accomplishments. This approach fit their organization and their culture.

David Smith's Top Tips for Global Facilitators:

- Rethink your online delivery techniques to adapt for the audience. For example, ask a question and instead of expecting everyone to respond verbally, say "If you're happy to speak out, please do, otherwise respond in the chat window."

- Slow down your rate of speech without sounding like you are "dumbing down" the content. Talk at an appropriate rate for clarity and understanding.

- Eliminate idioms and colloquial phrases from your vocabulary. These are difficult for non-native English speakers to translate. Instead, sanitize your language so that all will easily understand what you say.

David Smith is the Global Director for Virtual Learning Solutions at TMA World.

Use Clear Language

When hearing someone from another country speak our language, we often hear his or her accent. Yet virtual facilitators need to remember that when delivering a virtual training class to a global audience, they are usually the one who has the accent. Therefore, facilitators should take care to be concise, not use jargon or uncommon phrases, and to slow down their rate of speech.

Also, when saying participant names during class, virtual facilitators should learn the correct pronunciation and use it. Ask for pronunciation help if needed. A trick I use is to phonetically spell out each person's name on a blank sheet of paper I keep on my desk. This helps me remember how to correctly say each name during class.

"When facilitating a virtual class with an international audience, I speak slower and pause more. I am more strategic about checking in with participants, and invite them to provide feedback on my pace. For example, I'll ask them to 'click the green check if you would like for me to slow down.'"

—**Justin Patton, Master Facilitator, Yum! Brands**

Recognize Cultural Differences

By its very nature, delivering virtual training to a global audience will surface cultural disparities among participants. These can be as subtle as time zone differences or as magnified as how one chooses to interact in a breakout group setting. Virtual facilitators should keep their eyes and ears open during a session to pick up on these nuances and ensure that they don't get in the way of learning.

For example, it's normal for a widely dispersed audience to be joining at different times of their day. A facilitator who says "good morning" to everyone could immediately undermine their credibility if it's already afternoon or evening for most participants. Similarly, a facilitator who annotates a date on the whiteboard should recognize that some cultures write month/day/year, while others write day/month/year. Even this slight difference could create misunderstandings among participants who are trying to read the posted information.

Technology Issues for Global Training

All of the principles learned in chapters 6 and 7, about preparing participants and coordinating logistics, apply regardless of your participants' geographic location. However, several technology factors need to be emphasized when dealing with a global audience.

"By the time we offer a virtual training class to our global audience, we have worked hard on all of the details and worked through all of the challenges."

—Lucy Brown, Senior Training Manager,
Global Learning and Development, IHS

First, it's extra important to confirm that global participants have the minimum required technology to fully participate in virtual training. From adequate Internet bandwidth to appropriate hardware and software, ensure each person has what he needs. A participant should be able to easily connect to a session at the start and stay connected throughout.

While this seems to be common sense, it can be problematic for some international participants because internet bandwidth capacities vary widely from country to country. (Akamai, 2013) Even if the capacity is enough for one participant, if multiple participants join from the same office location, it's possible to overload the network or the system.

I found this out the hard way when I delivered several virtual training sessions with many participants from India joining each one. We tested the Internet bandwidth speeds prior to class, but during class, several participants struggled to stay connected to the session because they lost Internet connectivity. In hindsight, we failed to take into account the number of participants who would individually join from that specific office building. It overloaded their network and created problems.

In another class series I delivered with participants in South America, they received the pre-class communication that each person needed to connect individually from their own computer. However, they reserved a conference room and all gathered in it—each one bringing their own computer and VoIP headset. Again, the number of participants in the same room overloaded the office Internet connection, and most struggled to stay connected during class.

Fortunately, these instances are not as common as they once were because Internet connectivity is improving worldwide. Yet it still deserves mention as a potential roadblock to successful global virtual training.

"We have experienced bandwidth issues in certain markets, so we keep file sizes of our virtual training documents smaller to help out. We want to keep in mind our audience and how they will be connected. We also set up conference lines as backups just in case."

—Tara Welsh, Training Readiness Leader, Yum! Brands

The other technology concern is ensuring that participants have the appropriate hardware and software required to participate. I elaborated on technology essentials in chapter 3—what's unique about global participants are the potential compatibility concerns. For example, a global participant in Southeast Asia might be more likely to connect using a mobile device instead of a standalone computer (Ellis, 2012). And this workplace trend of using devices instead of a computer is expanding worldwide. In fact, Gartner Research predicts that by 2017, half of all employers will require employees to use their own computing devices in the workplace (Gartner, 2013). Unfortunately, at the present time, mobile devices do not allow learners to fully participate in an interactive virtual training class due to their limited functionality. Therefore, compatibility issues could interfere with a successful global virtual training rollout.

One way to overcome any technology concerns is to work with a local IT contact in each location who has intimate knowledge of participant equipment. If you have involved your IT department in the virtual training rollout, they should be able to guide global participants who may need extra assistance or additional items like a headset, borrowed computer, or help with a software download.

Also, most virtual classroom platforms have test links that should be sent to participants ahead of time. One of my favorite pre-class activities when working with a global audience (and using a perpetual classroom) is to ask participants to log in to the room at least 48 hours in advance and complete a simple introduction activity that can only be completed if an individual has connected by a compatible computer. For instance, I might have them type an introduction into an always-open chat window. Or respond to a few poll questions. By completing this type of activity in advance of the class, they get the experience of connecting to the virtual classroom and they begin to learn the platform tools.

One Organization's Story

IHS, a global information company, offers virtual training to its employees around the world. According to Senior Training Manager Lucy Brown, virtual training allows her team to reach managers in remote locations who might not be able to receive training otherwise. They also use virtual training to save on travel costs. The topics range from coaching to performance management to running effective meetings, and are typically one hour in length. The classes have been so well-received that some employees who do have opportunity to attend in-person training classes choose to attend the virtual ones instead. Lucy attributes many factors to the success of their global training initiative:

- They offer sessions in the early morning and late at night (U.S. time) to accommodate all global time zones.
- They make it easy for participants to connect. They thoroughly test out all technology ahead of time, and encourage participants to join sessions 20 minutes early. Their goal is 100 percent connectivity for all participants.

- They have a producer join nearly every virtual training session. The producer is available online to help in case of technical challenges.
- They ensure the content design is extremely interactive for participants. They use the full range of tools available in their virtual classroom platform. They want to have such an effective class that participants stay engaged the entire time.
- They have three virtual trainers, each one specializing in a few topics. This way, the trainers are both well-versed in the content and the virtual training platform.
- The virtual trainers extensively practice their delivery skills. Their goal is to be extremely comfortable in the online classroom. They also strive to be conversational with participants, so that the audience is able to learn and connect with the content.
- They connect with as many participants as they can ahead of time, to find out what questions and challenges participants have around the training topic. This way, the trainer can adjust the class as needed, to make it as relevant as possible.

Evaluation Considerations

At the start of your virtual training project, in chapter 2 of this book, I encouraged you to define your vision of success. You were asked to answer these questions:

"What's our goal for this training program? What are we trying to accomplish? What do we want to be different as a result of it? Do we need participants to be more knowledgeable about a topic? Do we want them to behave differently? Take action on something? How will our organization change or improve as a result? What's the best way to achieve these goals? How specifically would virtual training help achieve these outcomes?"

Evaluating the success of your virtual training is as simple as revisiting these questions to determine if you achieved your desired outcomes. Ask yourself and your team, "Did we accomplish our goal(s)?" Your response to this question can indicate success.

There are additional ways to evaluate the success of your virtual training. It's easiest to think about these evaluation considerations in terms of Kirkpatrick's widely used "levels of evaluation" model (2006):

- Level 1—Reactions

- Level 2—Learning
- Level 3—Behavior Change
- Level 4—Organizational Impact.

Level 1—Reaction

This first evaluation level considers participant reactions to the virtual training event, namely asking the question, "Did they like it?" These data are typically collected through an end-of-session questionnaire, and mostly conducted using an online survey tool. A Level 1 survey usually asks for opinions about the program content, the facilitator effectiveness, ease of using the platform tool, and for open-ended comments about the class.

A Level 1 evaluation could be expanded to include reactions of all stakeholders who were involved with the virtual training rollout. It could be very useful to find out their experience with and reaction to the event. For example, you might check in with the IT resources who conducted any pre-session tech checks to gather feedback on that process. Or you could ask those involved with the administrative logistics of your virtual training for their reactions and experience. In both cases, this evaluation data could contribute to your overall calculation of training success.

Collecting Level 1 data enables you to look for trends in participant reactions, which in turn could help you improve the program. In addition, these types of post-class reaction surveys are prime fodder for anecdotes and participant testimonials about a training curriculum. Positive quotes can be used in advertising materials for future programs.

Level 2—Learning

Level 2 evaluations measure if participants learned anything during the training program. When you include knowledge checks or quizzes in a virtual class, and track correct responses, you are measuring participant learning. A quiz could be conducted during class as an interactive activity and to check intermediary learning, yet it's most common to use an end-of-program quiz to fully measure knowledge learned.

Many virtual classroom platforms include a quizzing tool that can easily be used during or immediately after a training event to test for knowledge. Instructional designers would build these quiz questions into the program design. Alternatively, Level 2 questions are often combined together with Level 1 reaction surveys. Either way, the point of Level 2 evaluation is to find out what attendees actually learned by participating in the class. These data can be used to help measure the success of your training program because they demonstrate knowledge acquisition.

Level 3—Application

The next level of evaluation takes place several weeks after the training program, and measures whether or not participants are using the skills on the job. It requires deliberate effort to collect this information, either through observing participant actions, testing for on-the-job application, or measuring for qualitative data that can prove behavior change.

For example, let's say your virtual training curriculum centers around coaching skills for new managers. They learn techniques for setting goals with employees, and a process for holding performance conversations. To measure Level 3 application of these skills, you could spend time in the field with participants, shadowing them as they meet with their employees to set goals. You could use a rating scale based upon the specific skills learned during class to determine if the new managers are applying the goal-setting and conversational skills learned. Since this method is time consuming and potentially invasive to both the manager and employee, there are other ways to gather similar data. You could survey the manager and employee to ask about the process they used to set goals and whether or not the training skills were used during the performance discussion. You could also request anonymous access to a sampling of employee records to see the goals set during those meetings, and evaluate if they were accomplished.

Since Level 3 evaluations take place 30 to 60 days after a training event, one challenge is to show that it was participation in the training program that affected the behavior and not some other influencing factor, such as a water cooler conversation or some other on-the-job experience by the participant. Another challenge specific to virtual training is that your participants are typically geographically dispersed and therefore it can be more difficult to collect Level 3 observations. For this reason, surveys are much easier to use after virtual training events.

Regardless of how you collect Level 3 evaluation data, it's a key measure of the success of your virtual training program. The ability to demonstrate that participants are applying the skills learned and that your training program is having specific job impact on performance is a golden opportunity to evaluate success.

Level 4—Organizational Impact

The point of a Level 4 evaluation is to measure whether or not the virtual training program affected organizational results. It's the most difficult level to measure due to so many other influencing factors on business results. In fact, according to a 2009 ASTD study, only 36.9 percent of organizations even attempt to measure Level 4 data, as compared to 91.6 percent who use Level 1 evaluations (ASTD, 2009, 11). Even though measuring business results can be challenging, if you are able to determine that your virtual training curriculum had a positive impact on the organization, then by all means you should make the time and effort to complete a Level 4 evaluation. What better way to evaluate virtual training success than to show that it positively affected business results?

Finally, above and beyond Kirkpatrick's four levels of evaluation is what Jack Phillips has coined the fifth level: return-on-investment (ROI). The basic ROI calculation for a training program determines the difference between program costs and its net benefits, expressed as a percentage. Phillips's methodology actually goes beyond this simple measurement to more fully analyze ROI data. (For more information on this methodology, see one of his many books. My favorite is *Show Me the Money: How to Determine ROI in People, Projects, and Programs*). According to the same 2009 ASTD study on evaluation mentioned above, only 17.9 percent of organizations undertake ROI measurements (2009, 11). However, this small statistic should not deter your organization from considering it as a way to evaluate success.

Using any or all these evaluation techniques can help you measure the effectiveness of your virtual training program. So start planning your evaluation strategy at the beginning of your journey.

Future Considerations

Assuming that your virtual training project is wildly successful, and you plan to continue using live online training as a learning method, then there are several trends to keep an eye on. These three trends are sure to have impact on virtual training over the coming months and years:

- MOOCs and virtual learning environments

- mobile connectivity

- microbursts of learning.

MOOCs and Virtual Learning Environments

Over the past few years, the explosion of MOOCs (massive open online courses) has been hard to ignore. Most colleges and universities are jumping on the bandwagon to offer these types of online classes. MOOCs combine a variety of learning activities—video lectures, discussion boards, reading assignments, and exercises—to achieve prescribed learning outcomes. MOOCs typically draw a large audience (hence the descriptive word "massive"). We defined a MOOC back in chapter 2, saying that only if it included live online classes as an activity would we consider it to be related to our definition of virtual training.

A similar popular trend is the rise of "virtual learning environments," or VLEs for short. There are a few different types of VLEs, yet they can all be defined as a type of online platform that houses learning activities. A learning management system could be a type of VLE, if a participant logs in and sees a clear path of related learning activities to complete for a curriculum and can easily navigate to each activity. Other types of VLEs are more three-dimensional, like a video game screen, where a participant looks like a computerized character and navigates through the environment to engage in learning activities.

What's interesting to me, and the reason I believe MOOCs and VLEs are an important future trend to consider, is that they can place a single virtual training class into a larger context. In other words, a MOOC or VLE is in essence a type of blended training program that might include virtual training sessions as one component. At its core, a MOOC or VLE offers learning through a series of planned activities and events. If it's well designed, then a student who completes the series will achieve specific learning outcomes. Blended curriculums allow for the learning to take place over time, which can lead to better overall results. And virtual training classes can be key components of an effective blended program.

All of the principles outlined in this book apply to all types of virtual training—whether an individual session or a series of live online events. And if your virtual training events are offered as a blended curriculum as part of a MOOC or VLE, you would still use the tips and techniques suggested here. However, if you design, deliver, or implement virtual training, be prepared to increase your scope beyond single events. Virtual training fits well with MOOCs and VLEs and you may be asked to work with larger blended curriculums.

Mobile Connectivity

Several times in this book, I have cautioned against using mobile devices for facilitating (and even attending) virtual training. This recommendation is largely based on the limited functionality of current apps that are now available for virtual classroom platforms. For example, one popular platform has a mobile app for its "meeting" product but not it's "training" product. Another popular platform has a mobile app, but it only includes certain features such as viewing slides and typing in chat. It's typical that when using mobile virtual classroom apps, participants cannot respond to polls, annotate on the screen, or use many other common tools available in the standard computer version.

My hope and expectation is that the features and functionality of mobile device apps for virtual classroom platforms will increase, and soon. As devices get more sophisticated, and apps are developed for live online training, we are certain to see an increased usage of mobile devices for virtual training. The proliferation of mobile devices in the workplace will drive this trend.

In the future, participants will be able to easily connect via their tablet or phone and have full functionality of an interactive virtual training event. Facilitators will be able to effortlessly deliver sessions in the same way. The mobile apps will be robust enough to handle everything a facilitator needs to do. Likewise, mobile data speeds will be strong enough to handle the connectivity needs of a virtual training class. Therefore, it will be important for you to stay abreast of changes in mobile device capability and to be prepared for this change.

Microbursts of Learning

Almost everything seems to be trending towards "shorter" and "faster" these days. For example, many people have moved from postal mail to email to text messaging. Likewise, many individuals who started with website blogging have now moved onto social media microblogging. And popular online videos used to be a few minutes in length, but now they are often only a few seconds in length. These illustrative examples mirror the trends of "shorter" and "faster" that affect many aspects of our lives.

In a similar fashion, the amount of time that most organizations allot for training events has decreased over the years. How many of us remember commonly hosting three-, four-, and five-day classes (or longer!) on a regular basis? While many organizations still offer these lengthy classes for topics that require it, most organizations are looking for ways to trim training costs and shorten the amount of time spent in the classroom. So instead of scheduling a two-day class, training departments are asked to schedule a one-day class. Or instead of a one-day class, they are asked to make it a half-day one.

The good news is that virtual training is ideally poised to meet the trend of shorter and faster training classes. In many ways it is already filling that need due to its typical 60- to 90-minute length. However, in the future, I believe we will see even shorter classes, or what I would consider to be a "microburst" of learning. You could think of it as a "mini-class" due to its shortened length.

In this context, a virtual training microburst could be a 10- to 15-minute live online session covering a single topic or learning objective. Or, a virtual training microburst could be an open question-and-answer session with a subject matter expert. Or it could be just one small activity in the context of a series, such as a mini-session in a blended curriculum. Each microburst would be bite-sized for quick learning consumption.

Just as we have seen the trend to shorten traditional training classes, we will see the trend to shorten virtual training classes. It will create challenges for designers who must resist the temptation to cram too much content into a microburst session. And it will create delivery and implementation challenges as organizations figure out how to schedule these events in ways that make sense to participants and facilitators. Despite these challenges, it's a trend to watch.

In fact, your organization may decide to be a trendsetter and implement all three of these things now, at the beginning of your virtual training journey. It's an exciting time to be involved with live online learning.

References

Akamai. (2013). "State of the Internet Report." www.akamai.com/stateoftheinternet/.

ASTD. (2012). *Mobile Learning: Delivering Learning in a Connected World*. Alexandria, VA: ASTD Press.

ASTD. (2012). *State of the Industry*. Alexandria, VA: ASTD Press.

ASTD. (2009). *The Value of Evaluation: Making Training Evaluations More Effective*. Alexandria, VA: ASTD Press.

Babson College. (2012). "2012 Survey of Online Learning" Babson College, www.babson. edu/news-events/babson-news/pages/130107-2012-survey-of-online-learning-results. aspx.

Baker, C. (2010). "The Impact of Instructor Immediacy and Presence for Online Student Affective Learning, Cognition, and Motivation." *The Journal of Educators Online*, volume 7, number 1.

BBC News. (2008, May 30). "Formula 'Secret of Perfect Voice.'" *BBC News*, http://news. bbc.co.uk/2/hi/uk/7426923.stm.

Broad, M.L., and J.W. Newstrom. (1992). *Transfer of Training: Action-Packed Strategies to Ensure High Payoff From Training Investments*. Reading, MA: Addison-Wesley.

Chief Learning Officer. (2012, December 13). "Survey: Most Plan to Increase Virtual Learning in 2013." *Chief Learning Officer, Solutions for Enterprise Productivity*, http:// clomedia.com/articles/view/survey-most-plan-to-increase-virtual-learning-in-2013.

Christopher, D. (2012, February 1). "Keeping Participants' Attention in Global Virtual Classrooms," http://www.astd.org/Publications/Newsletters/Learning-Circuits/ Learning-Circuits-Archives/2012/02/Keeping-Participants-Attention-in-Global-Virtu-al-Classrooms. Adapted from "Facilitating in the Global Virtual Classroom," *Infoline* No. 1111 (November, 2011). Alexandria, VA: ASTD Press.

Clark, R.C., and A. Kwinn. (2007). *The New Virtual Classroom*. San Francisco: Pfeiffer.

Courville, R. (2012) Survey conducted via website, www.thevirtualpresenter.com.

Covey, S. (1989). *The 7 Habits of Highly Effective People: Powerful Lessons in Personal Change*. New York: Free Press.

Dirksen, J. (2012). *Design for How People Learn*. Berkeley, CA: New Riders.

Eddy, N. (2012, January 6). "Mobile Worker Population to Reach 1.3 Billion by 2015: IDC." *eWEEK*, www.eweek.com/c/a/Mobile-and-Wireless/Mobile-Worker-Population-to-Reach-13-Billion-by-2015-IDC-238980/.

Ellis, R.K. (2012, December 5). "Accenture Study Details Digital's Disruptive Impact on Workforce in Southeast Asia" www.astd.org/Publications/Blogs/Global-HRD-Blog/2012/12/Accenture-Study-Details-Digitals-Disruptive-Impact-on-Workforce-in-Southeast-Asia.

ESPN. (2010). "John Wooden's Greatest Quotes." *ESPN: The Worldwide Leader In Sports*, http://sports.espn.go.com/ncb/news/story?id=5249709.

Falloon, G. (2011, December). "Exploring the Virtual Classroom: What Students Need to Know (and Teachers Should Consider)." *Journal of Online Learning and Teaching*, volume. 7, number 4.

Gartner Research. (2013, May 1). "Gartner Predicts by 2017, Half of Employers Will Require Employees to Supply Their Own Device for Work Purposes." *Technology Research*, Gartner Inc., www.gartner.com/newsroom/id/2466615.

Huggett, C. (2010). *Virtual Training Basics*. Alexandria, VA: ASTD Press.

Jacobs School of Engineering. (2013, January 30). "Working Alone Won't Get You Good Grades." UCSD Jacobs School of Engineering, www.jacobsschool.ucsd.edu/news/news_releases/release.sfe?id=1308.

Jaschik, S. (2009, June 29). "The Evidence on Online Education." *Inside Higher Ed*, www.insidehighered.com/news/2009/06/29/online.

Kalman, F. (2011, October). "Training is Essential for Successful Telework Management." *Chief Learning Officer magazine*, http://clomedia.com/articles/view/flexible-work-arrangements-require-clo-involvement-to-shift-mindsets/3. (Original research from Dieringer Research Group and WorldatWork.)

Kirkpatrick, D.L., and J.D. Kirkpatrick. (2006). *Evaluating Training Programs: The Four Levels (3rd edition)*. San Francisco: Berrett-Koehler.

Laird, D. (1985). *Approaches To Training And Development (2nd ed.)*. Reading, MA: Addison-Wesley.

Landry, L. (2013, January 8). "Over 6.7 Million Students Are Now Taking Classes Online." *Bostlnno*, http://bostinno.com/2013/01/08/2012-babson-survey-of-online-learning-6-7-million-students-taking-classes-online/#ss__281086_1_0__ss.

Martin, F., M.A. Parker, and D.F. Deale. (2012). "Examining Interactivity in Virtual Classrooms." *The International Review of Research in Open and Distance Learning*, volume 13, number 3, www.irrodl.org/index.php/irrodl/article/view/1174/2253.

Medina, J. (2008). *Brain Rules*. Seattle: Pear Press. (2010).

Mervis, J. (2011, May 12). "A Better Way to Teach?" *Science*, http://news.sciencemag.org/sciencenow/2011/05/a-better-way-to-teach.html.

Mina, A. (2012, October 9). "Virtual Training: Tips to Reduce Budget Without Sacrificing Engagement." *GP Strategies*, http://blog.gpstrategies.com/learning-content/virtual-training-improve-engagement.

Murdoch, M., and T. Muller. (2013). *The Webinar Manifesto: Never Design, Deliver, or Sell Lousy Webinars Again*. New York: RosettaBooks.

Pike, R.W. (2002). *Creative Training Techniques Handbook, (3rd ed.)*. Amherst, MA: HRD Press.

Pike, R.W. (2011). "Creative Training Techniques for Webinars: Seven Ways to Add Impact and Wow—NOW!" Session presented at ASTD TechKnowledge® 2011 Conference & Exposition, San Jose, CA, February 2011.

Pink, D.H. (2012). *To Sell Is Human: The Surprising Truth About Moving Others*. New York: Riverhead Books.

Phillips, J.J., and P.P. Phillips. (2007). *Show Me the Money*. San Francisco: Berrett-Koehler Publishers.

Rossett, A. and R.V. Frazee. (2006). AMA Special Report "Blended Learning Opportunities." American Management Association.

Shank, P. (2010). "Getting Started with Synchronous e-Learning" The eLearning Guild.

Silverman, R.E. (2012, December 12). "Workplace Distractions: Here's Why You Won't Finish This Article." *Wall Street Journal*, http://online.wsj.com/article/SB10001424127887324339204578173252223022388.html. (Original research done by Stanford University.)

Towards Maturity. (2011). "Harnessing Live Online Learning: The UK's First Research Study Into Virtual Learning." *Towards Maturity*, www.cloud4training.com.

United States Census Bureau. (2010). 2010 Census Report, www.census.gov/2010census/.

Westerman, G. (2012, April 2). "IT Is From Venus, Non-IT Is From Mars." *Wall Street Journal*, page R2.

Wikipedia. (2013). "List of Most Popular Given Names," http://en.wikipedia.org/wiki/List_of_most_popular_given_names.

Resources

Books

I encourage you to continue learning about designing, delivering, and implementing virtual training. If you are interested in diving deeper into the topics covered in this book, then here are a few resources from my own bookshelf that I recommend.

Biech, E. (2005). *Training for Dummies.* Hoboken, NJ; Wiley.

Bozarth, J. (2013). *Better Than Bullet Points: Creating Engaging e-Learning with PowerPoint,* (2nd ed.). San Francisco: Pfeiffer.

Brandon, B. (editor). (2008). *144 Tips on Synchronous Learning Strategy + Research.* Available at www.elearningguild.com.

Brandon, B. (editor). (2008). *The eLearning Guild's Handbook on Synchronous e-Learning.* Available at www.elearningguild.com.

Carnes, B. (2013). *Making eLearning Stick: Techniques for Easy and Effective Transfer of Technology-Supported Training.* Alexandria, VA: ASTD Press.

Carliner, S. (2001). *Training Design Basics.* Alexandria, VA: ASTD Press.

Christopher, D. (November 2011). "Facilitating in the Global Virtual Classroom," *Infoline* No. 1111, Alexandria, VA: ASTD Press.

Clark, R.C., and A. Kwinn. (2007). *The New Virtual Classroom: Evidence-Based Guidelines for Synchronous e-Learning.* San Francisco: Pfeiffer.

Clay, C. (2012). *Great Webinars: How to Create Interactive Learning That Is Captivating, Informative and Fun.* San Francisco: Pfeiffer.

Corbett, W.G. and C. Huggett. (2009) "Designing for the Virtual Classroom," *Infoline* No. 0911, Alexandria, VA: ASTD Press.

Cross, J. and L. Dublin. (2002). *Implementing E-Learning.* Alexandria, VA: ASTD Press.

Courville, R. (2009). *The Virtual Presenter's Handbook*. CreateSpace Independent Publishing Platform. Available at www.thevirtualpresenter.com.

Dirksen, J. (2012). *Design for How People Learn*. Berkeley, CA: New Riders.

Hodell, C. (2011). *ISD From the Ground Up: A Non-Nonsense Approach to Instructional Design*. Alexandria, VA: ASTD Press.

Hofmann, J. (2004). *Live and Online!: Tips, Techniques, and Ready-to-Use Activities for the Virtual Classroom*. San Francisco: Pfeiffer.

Hofmann, J. (2004). *The Synchronous Trainer's Survival Guide: Facilitating Successful Live and Online Courses, Meetings, and Events*. San Francisco: Pfeiffer.

Hofmann, J. and N. Miner. (2009). *Tailored Learning: Designing the Blend that Fits*. Alexandria, VA; ASTD Press.

Hubbard, Rob (2013) *The Really Useful eLearning Instruction Manual: Your toolkit for putting eLearning into Practice*. San Francisco, CA: Wiley.

Huggett, Cindy. (2010). *Virtual Training Basics*. Alexandria, VA: ASTD Press.

Huggett, Cindy and Wendy Gates Corbett. (2009) "Simple, Effective, Online Training" *Infoline* No. 0801, Alexandria, VA: ASTD Press.

Kirkpatrick, D.L., and J.D. Kirkpatrick. (2006). *Evaluating Training Programs: The Four Levels* (3rd edition). San Francisco: Berrett-Koehler.

Koegel, T.J. (2010). *The Exceptional Presenter Goes Virtual*. Austin: Greenleaf Press.

McClay, R. and L. Irwin. (2008). *The Essential Guide to Training Global Audiences: Your Planning Resource of Useful Tips and Techniques*. San Francisco: Pfeiffer

Murdoch, M. and T. Muller. (2013). *The Webinar Manifesto: Never Design, Deliver, or Sell Lousy Webinars Again*. New York: RosettaBooks.

Pink, D.H. (2012). *To Sell Is Human: The Surprising Truth About Moving Others*. New York: Riverhead Books.

Phillips, J.J., and P.P. Phillips. (2007). *Show Me the Money*. San Francisco: Berrett-Koehler.

Phillips, J.J., and P.P. Phillips. (2005). *Return on Investment (ROI) Basics*. Alexandria, VA: ASTD Press.

Phillips, P.P. (editor). (2010). *ASTD Handbook of Measuring and Evaluating Training*. Alexandria, VA: ASTD Press.

Pike, R.W. (2002). *Creative Training Techniques Handbook,* (3rd ed.). Amherst, MA: HRD Press.

Pluth, B.P. (2010). *Webinars with WOW Factor: Tips, Tricks and Interactive Activities for Virtual Training.* Minneapolis: Pluth Consulting.

Reynolds, G. (2008). *Presentation Zen: Simple Ideas on Presentation Design and Delivery.* (2nd ed.) Berkeley, CA: New Riders.

Russell, L. (2007). *10 Steps to Successful Project Management.* Alexandria, VA: ASTD Press.

Scannell, M., M. Abrhams and M. Mulvihill. *Big Book of Virtual Team Building Games: Quick, Effective Activities to Build Communication Trust and Collaboration from Anywhere.* (2011). New York: McGraw-Hill.

Steed, C. (2011). *Facilitating Live Online Learning.* Engaged Online Learning. Available at www.colinsteed.com.

Shank, P. (2010). *Getting Started with Synchronous e-Learning.* Santa Rosa, CA: The eLearning Guild (available at www.elearningguild.com).

Shank, P. (2011). *The Online Learning Idea Book: Proven Ways to Enhance Technology-Based and Blended Learning, Volume Two.* San Francisco: Pfeiffer.

Turmel, W. (2011). *10 Steps to Successful Virtual Presentations.* Alexandria, VA: ASTD Press.

Udell, C. (2012). *Learning Everywhere: How Mobile Content Strategies Are Transforming Training.* Nashville, TN: Rockbench Publishing.

A Selected List of Virtual Classroom Software Vendors

Here are a few examples of common virtual classroom software platforms. Please note that this is not an exhaustive list, nor does it imply endorsement of any particular vendor.

Adobe Connect:

www.adobe.com/products/adobeconnect

Blackboard Collaborate:

www.blackboard.com/platforms/collaborate/overview.aspx

Cisco WebEx Training Center:

www.webex.com/products/elearning-and-online-training.html

Citrix GoToTraining:

www.gototraining.com

Saba Classroom:

www.sabameeting.com/mar/virtual-classroom-software

Trademark Attributions

Adobe, Flash, and Adobe Connect are either registered trademarks or trademarks of Adobe Systems Incorporated in the United States and/or other countries.

Cisco WebEx Meeting Center, Event Center, Training Center and Support Center are trademarks of Cisco Systems, Inc. and/or one or more of its subsidiaries, and may be registered in the United States Patent and Trademark Office and in other countries.

Citrix GoToMeeting, GoToWebinar, and GoToTraining are trademarks of Citrix Systems, Inc. and/or one or more of its subsidiaries, and may be registered in the United States Patent and Trademark Office and in other countries.

Microsoft, Microsoft Office, and Windows Media Player are either registered trademarks or trademarks of Microsoft Corporation in the United States and/or other countries.

About the Author

 Cindy Huggett, CPLP, is an independent consultant, professional speaker, instructional designer, classroom facilitator, and author who specializes in workplace training and development. With more than 20 years of professional experience, Cindy has successfully designed curriculums, facilitated classes, and led training rollouts in almost every industry and every size organization.

Cindy partners with her clients to help them transition to the virtual classroom. She also facilitates, designs, writes, and speaks on topics related to leadership, virtual training, and learning. She is the author of *Virtual Training Basics* (2010), and the co-author of two ASTD Press *Infolines*, "Simple, Effective Online Learning" (2008) and "Designing for the Virtual Classroom" (2009).

She holds a master's degree in Public and International Affairs from the University of Pittsburgh, and a bachelor's degree from James Madison University. Cindy was also one of the first training professionals to earn the Certified Professional in Learning and Performance (CPLP) designation.

Cindy's passion in life is helping others achieve success both personally and professionally. Her leadership roles and extracurricular activities are centered on this pursuit. She served on the national ASTD Board of Directors in 2009-2010. She was recognized by the *Triangle Business Journal* as a "40-Under-40" Award recipient and she co-founded a non-profit organization to promote volunteering and community service. She's also a Registered Yoga Teacher. This book continues her passion to help others, with hope that all who read it achieve greater success with their virtual training.

You can find Cindy online at www.cindyhuggett.com or sharing training tips on Twitter as @cindyhugg.

Index